conjectures

conjectures

conjectures
living with questions

by

James Leatt

WIPF & STOCK · Eugene, Oregon

CONJECTURES
Living with Questions

Wipf & Stock
An Imprint of Wipf and Stock Publishers
199 W. 8th Ave., Suite 3
Eugene, OR 97401

www.wipfandstock.com

PAPERBACK ISBN: 978-1-6667-5665-4
HARDCOVER ISBN: 978-1-6667-5666-1
EBOOK ISBN: 978-1-6667-5667-8

to those who question

CONTENTS

I would rather have questions that can't be answered
than answers that can't be questioned.
– Richard Feynman

Preface

No veneer. This desk of mine is the real thing. Crafted in solid blackwood in a workshop in Cape Town from a tree felled in a forest in Gauteng, I love the feel of it, its rich, grainy golden brown colour. It's here that I write the story of my own quest for answers, of my learning to be silent before the questions. And I want it to be the real thing, not a thin covering, a semblance of the real thing. No veneer.

I want this to be a non-jargon book that explores what spirituality means in a secular world. Thinking of my readers, I have in mind people like my friends and acquaintances of all ages who find they can no longer adhere to the tenets of Christianity but do not want to sacrifice their spirituality. People who want to live meaningfully and ethically but without the comforts and consolations of organised religion.

The story links my personal experience of growing up and living in South Africa during a troubling time in world history with my intellectual searching. It's about the courage I found to change my mind as the 'truths' that had guided me before were tested against contemporary experience. It is also about my growing incredulousness at totalising systems of all kinds.

It is autumn. A light breeze rustles the leaves of the poplars outside my study window. My home is on the edge of an eco-sensitive wetland in a newly established village in the wooded suburb of Hout Bay. Here sprawling shacks and extreme poverty live cheek by jowl with great wealth, enclosed in some fourteen walled-off gated estates.

In the distance, I can see traffic at the start of another working day. The lights of Imizama Yethu – IY as the locals call it – flicker in the distance. IY, also known as Mandela Park, is a sprawling, overcrowded, under-resourced informal settlement, testimony to the fact that people vote with their feet, calculating that their life chances are better here than they are in Zimbabwe, Malawi, the Congo, the Eastern Cape of South Africa, Namibia or the CAR. People living here are seeking a better life, and for that they have left behind parents, siblings, husbands, wives. Many are unemployed and daily make their pilgrimage to one or other intersection in Hout Bay, looking for work. I meet them on my early morning walks. Hout Bay is a microcosm of South Africa, 2014. I'm immersed in this reality, have been all my life, trying to make sense of it all.

For a long time apartheid masked the fault line that runs through South Africa. And in our naiveté we thought that if we could get rid of apartheid, all would be well. But of course our post-apartheid country now grapples with endemic poverty, unemployment and the harsh realities of racism and xenophobia.

Growing up in South Africa tests your mettle. For those, like me, who were born here in the late 1930s, a world recession, a world war, the Holocaust, and the long reach of colonialism and apartheid all tested our knowledge, taken-for-granted assumptions, often fondly held, and our faith. It was a crucible where context and ideas, events and beliefs, experiences and ideologies were mixed to make the stuff of history. Few, if any, have emerged unchanged. Certainly my foundations were profoundly shaken.

Like many white South Africans, I was sheltered from the harsh realities of my own country when I was growing up. Anything that had to do with the tireless struggles of black South Africans to make their case for a place in the sun alongside us whites had been edited out of school history books. It was only when I became a lay preacher working in the sprawling black areas of Cape Town that I was exposed to the crippling poverty, unemployment and structural violence wrought by the racist policies of our succeeding governments.

I have the distinct sense that several different people are the subject of this exercise in retrieval and reflection. All of them are named James Leatt, but they are assembled differently with each passing phase: the schoolboy who attended eleven different primary schools because his father kept losing his job; the lonely youngster who was somehow receptive to a 'signal of transcendence' that affirmed him at a low point in his life; the youth leader who sought to pass on his Christian faith to his fellow teens; the earnest pastor who spent his twenty-first birthday preaching to a packed marquee of displaced Coloured people at an evangelical mission in Retreat on the Cape Flats; the probationer minister in a dog collar leading a campaign to boost the finances of a middle-class white congregation in Bellville. They all answer to the name James Leatt. He is the same person whose foundations were shaken and whose vistas were opened up at Rhodes University. He is all that and more …

Brother, husband, father, grandfather. Avid reader, keen sportsman, reluctant attender of the local gym, fledgling wood turner, lover of good wine and enthusiastic member of the motorhome club – all these are James, too. You can find them nested inside, like a Russian matryoshka doll.

Ordained minister, college and university lecturer, professor, deputy vice chancellor, vice chancellor, between-jobs man, consultant, mentor and writer – you might say a wonderfully varied career or an example of poor career planning. James Leatt is all these people and none of them. Until my memory falters, I can retrieve episodes from all of them.

Writing now, decades later, I know that they all contribute to my identity. Who am I? Like Tennyson's Ulysses 'I am part of all that I have met.' And yet, thanks to the brain's plasticity, I am ever-evolving, changing, growing – open to new experiences. For anticipation, too, is a *present* experience. I live *between* memory and anticipation.

But why write? Who is interested in my story? There's a 'two-million-year-old self in all of us,' says Jung. What if telling my story is in some sense telling the story of humankind? That's neither trivial nor presumptuous. What Jung is saying is that our roots lie in archaic humankind. Trying to reflect in a disciplined way on my own journey is somehow to replay an ancient story of the struggle described by neuroscientists as the 'Four Fs': feeding, fighting, fleeing and – for want of a more basic word – mating. The struggle not only to give these drives appropriate expression, but also to move beyond them. And in doing so, to make sense of the world, to become less alienated from my own humanity.

> I live my life in widening circles
> that reach out across the world.
> I may not complete this last one
> but I give myself to it.
>
> I circle around God, around the primordial tower.
> I've been circling for thousands of years
> and I still don't know: am I a falcon,
> a storm, or a great song?
>
> – Rainer Maria Rilke, 'Widening Circles'

Private dreams and myths are part of this story. What ails me ails humanity. What challenges me is our challenge too. So, it's not presumptuous to write about my 'memories, dreams and reflections', in Carl Jung's words, if what comes out is a story you can tell around a campfire, particular enough to be my story, yet wide enough to warm those gathering around the fire. My story is a 'useful fiction' others may identify with, a proxy for others' struggles to find themselves.

The way I see it, mine is not a story about the loss of faith so much as about how my mind has changed, what the issues were that shook my foundations, and the place I have reached in my searching. And in this endeavour I know I am not alone. A sampling of my own bookshelves bears testimony to this universal searching. There is a slim book by the French philosopher André Comte-Sponville, called

4

The Book of Atheist Spirituality (2006). Elegantly written for the lay public, it tackles the questions we have all asked: Can we do without religion? Does God exist? Can there be an atheist spirituality?

Another, by Ronald Aronson, a Professor of the History of Ideas at Wayne State University is called *Living Without God: New Directions for Atheists, Agnostics, Secularists and the Undecided* (2008). Aronson makes the argument that atheism is more than what one does *not* believe – it is the precondition for a 'generous humanism', which he then tries to articulate.

Then there's this beautifully produced hardcover volume edited by Louise Antony, Professor of Philosophy at the University of Massachusetts, Amherst. It's called *Philosophers Without Gods: Meditations on Atheism and the Secular Life* (2007). She's collected the personal reflections of nineteen leading philosophers. Many of the essays describe the personal journeys of these scholars from their roots in Judaism or Christianity to a secular or atheist position.

As Antony says, atheism is a minority stance in today's world. In those parts of the globe accessible to surveys, most people believe in God. Her collection of essays is intended to provide a peek at the personal and intellectual grapplings of scholars who have rejected religious orthodoxy but who take religion seriously.

Secularists or humanists or atheists, or any combination of these, they write about why they have given up religious belief for a naturalistic understanding of the human condition that reveals a set of heroic challenges – in Antony's words: 'to pursue our goals without illusions, to act morally without hope of reward – challenges that, if taken up, impart a durable value to finite and fragile human lives.'

I am *not* an atheist. But I can no longer subscribe to the doctrines and practices of orthodox Christianity. I don't think my journey is unique. I want to try to explain how I got to a naturalistic understanding of the human condition myself, one not explained by, or dependent in any way on, the supernatural. And I want to

5

try to convey what it means to live morally and meaningfully, even reverently, in a world without gods.

When I'm using the word 'God' in my writing, I'm mostly referring to the radically transcendent God of the Abrahamic family of religions or, more popularly, the notion of a supernatural agent active in the world of nature and human experience. But I am also sceptical of *any* capitalisation of an idea, ideology, authority, person, place or thing.

And when I use the word 'gods', I am talking about *any* idea, system, person, community or ideology (religious or secular) to which I'm expected to give my allegiance, to submit to its claims.

I am interested in trying to say something meaningful about complex and slippery words that embed human experience. How to understand religion? What to make of the 'silence of God'? How does the language game of 'secular spirituality' work? What are you if you are not a theist or a deist, but don't want to espouse modern atheism? What does 'living without gods' entail?

Interlude

Most books are rooted in biography.
– Peter Berger

I grew up as the oldest of three children in the Leatt household in the 1940s and 1950s. We struggled. My immigrant father was often unemployed. There were times when we could have ended up as 'poor whites' were it not for the generosity of my mother's family. They subsidised us, especially when my parents were on an alcoholic binge.

It took me a long time to understand that my mother and father were dealing with their own ghosts as best they could – years of counselling to understand that parenthood is over-rated. By that I mean I would cede too much to my parents if I acted as though their errors had irrevocably shaped my life. I discovered that when I stop playing the blame game, I remain open to discovering my *daimon*. As James Hillman says, the 'parental fallacy is deadly to individual self-awareness'.

There are some shadows you cannot move. My parents' addiction to alcohol is one. My father was born in a London workhouse in 1896. He was the victim of mustard gas poisoning in the First World War, which enduringly impaired his health. He immigrated to South Africa as a young man with no post-secondary education. In 1937, he married my mother, who had recently ended a disastrous marriage. In the harsh economic climate of the times, he was often a casualty of the 'last in first out' principle. As a result we moved around the country in search of work and I attended more than my share of primary schools, around a dozen.

My mother was of the 1820 Settlers stock and grew up in the comfort of a wealthy Kimberley home. But I believe she saw herself as one of life's victims, always drawing the short straw. By her own admission, her drinking worsened over the years, especially after my father died in 1966. My memories of her are coarse-grained. On more than one occasion, I had to commit her for treatment because she refused to acknowledge that she was an alcoholic. Never a pleasant experience, especially for a child.

Another shadow I cannot move is the Holocaust. I was eleven … at my cousin John's ninth birthday party. His father, Uncle Elkan, was performing conjuring tricks. Then we watched reels of films, hired from the British Consulate, on a Kodak projector. The main feature was a Charlie Chaplin movie. But had Uncle looked at the supporting programme before?

My uncle was out of the room. In the dark, we watched a black and white short showing Allied troops liberating the Belsen and Dachau concentration camps. On his return, he stopped the film, muttering an apology. He hastily threaded the Charlie Chaplin movie, which we watched twice, and laughed until tears rolled down our cheeks.

Even today I still break out in a cold sweat at the graphic images of skeletal figures stacked on top of each other in hastily dug holes, emaciated men and women staring out from behind barbed-wire fences, and inert bodies left where they fell. And the look of utter horror on the faces of the Allied troops as they entered the camps.

At age eleven, I came face to face with 'the problem of evil'. A picture is worth a thousand words. Many thousands of words have been written to address this problem. I have read a great number of them. But I have yet to find an adequate way of dealing with how 'God' could have 'allowed' the concentration camps. What God could have let that happen?

After Belsen, Dachau, Auschwitz, what is the meaning of good, of God? I will return to this theme often in this book. For many of my generation, the Holocaust is unique, a defining moment. It represents both the depths of depravity and the 'banality of evil', in Hannah Arendt's famous words. It challenges fundamentally the way you view the world.

But there were also moments of transcendence. In my late teens, I was standing on the veranda of our rented house in Kalk Bay late one night. I was desperate. We had little money. My parents were drunk, and there was no food in the house.

Yet, as I looked up at the stars, it was as if I could touch them. Then out of somewhere a voice said 'you are a child of the universe, you have a right to be here'. An overwhelming sense of wellbeing and peace came over me.

In that brief moment, I felt that I had received some kind of 'signal of transcendence'. I didn't hear the voice of God. What I felt was the sense of being connected with all that is. Difficult to explain, but as real as butter.

At the time, I interpreted my Kalk Bay experience within the framework of Protestant Christianity of the Methodist variety. My parents were nominally Methodists. I had attended Sunday school and been confirmed in the local Methodist church, in Muizenberg. I believed in a personal God who loves His children. Only much later did I discover that the words that came to me that night are from the prose poem 'Desiderata' by the American writer Max Ehrmann:

> … be gentle with yourself.
> You are a child of the universe,
> no less than the trees and the stars;
> You have a right to be here.

9

It was not long after this experience that I was roundly converted. Our church was holding an outreach mission and I was helping out as a member of the youth group. One night, Ruth Cook, who was leading the proceedings, asked a question that got through to me: 'What happens when you turn on a light switch?' Suddenly, I had the answer … 'Well,' said Ruth, 'that's what happens when you accept Christ as your personal saviour. The darkness in your life is dispelled.' That did it. Another 'signal of transcendence'. I became a committed Christian at age sixteen. My father, as ever, was sceptical. He hated cant and hypocrisy. My friends were wary. Our local pastor and his wife were delighted and supportive. The church, with its lively youth group, became my focal point.

Later, I became a lay preacher and successfully sat for the Methodist Church of South Africa examinations. I enjoyed my active role in the church, yet could never be sure what awaited me when I got home from some exhilarating church activity. Never simple to leave a drunken home for a preaching assignment. Always ill at ease, I was.

You could say of the religion of my teens that I projected onto God all the needs I had for a father who cared. One of my enduring memories of my own father is the tongue lashings he meted out to me when he was drunk. I have never known anyone as skilful at finding fault. The way we talk to our children becomes their inner critic. And mine was severe. You could say that I 'used' religion to survive and adapt during my teen years, when I bore the burden of a troubled family. You could say that the local Methodist church became the loving family I didn't have. Methodism meant the world to me. I especially loved the singing – Methodism was born in song – and the vibrancy of the services.

I felt welcomed in a community of belonging. I had a Father I could rely on, and a faith to carry me through troubled times. John Wesley, the founder of Methodism, was once saved from a burning house. He described himself as 'a brand plucked from the burning'. And that's how I felt – saved and safe in the arms of the Church.

I planned to leave school in Standard Eight, thinking to supplement the family income. My father argued from his own experience of the labour market: 'Without a matric your prospects will be poor.' And so I stayed.

When I matriculated, I joined Barclays Bank and looked forward to a career in banking. This was not to be. I was approached by the Order of Christian Service (OCS), a non-profit organisation dedicated to putting young people into the field for periods of service. I joined the OCS in the late 1950s to serve as a lay pastor in the Diep River and Kenilworth Circuit of the Methodist Church. The cluster of churches in that circuit all served Coloured South Africans. Some were in poor areas, like Retreat and Grassy Park; others were in more well-to-do suburbs, like Wynberg. I was living on a 'stipend', a living allowance paid from OCS donor funds, and working in what were then called Coloured 'group areas' of the southern Cape Peninsula.

I plunged into this new world with trepidation. Would the congregations accept me? I was barely twenty years of age, white and woefully inexperienced. My understanding of race relations was that of most English-speaking white South Africans in the late 1950s – I had hardly had any contact with black South Africans. This fish had attended all-white schools, lived in white suburbs and swallowed the white-and-English-language-bias of my school curriculum, hook, line and sinker. I hadn't heard of the African National Congress (ANC) or the South African Communist Party (SACP), and had never read the Freedom Charter. Though Nelson Mandela and other stalwarts would soon be imprisoned on Robben Island a few kilometres away, I knew little about their struggle for freedom and justice. I knew nothing about the complexities of race politics.

I spent my twenty-first birthday preaching on a hot February day in a tent mission at a new housing estate in Retreat. I wonder at my audacity, even rashness, preaching to large crowds assembled in a giant marquee. But I felt called, and wasn't I standing in a tradition going back to the 1700s and John and Charles Wesley, who took to open-air preaching to reach the masses?

The years I spent as an OCS pastor convinced me of my calling to the ministry. The 1960 Conference of the Methodist Church accepted me as a probationer with six years of training ahead – three years under supervision in a circuit and three at Rhodes University. The Church recognised my OCS work and posted me to the Bellville congregation of the Metropolitan Circuit.

Taking leave of the folks in the Diep River and Kenilworth circuit was hard. I'd cut my eyeteeth there. I'd been with the people when they married, when their children were born and when they died. I have a flashback of Mr Cyster, an elderly man riddled with cancer and writhing in pain. His family looking helplessly on. Pain management wasn't what it is today. I'd tried to help them understand the rudiments of the Christian faith when they were confirmed. I'd lived through the trials and tribulations of people who were marginalised politically. The application of the Group Areas Act had robbed many of their properties in the Diep River, Wynberg and Kenilworth suburbs. The application of the Mixed Marriages Act had torn many of their families asunder.

I was quite unprepared for the experience of confronting apartheid at the coalface, where it affected people not only morally but also materially. As a white South African, apartheid had little or no direct negative effect on me in this respect. But in the communities I served it left only devastation in its stead. The church seemed powerless in the face of it all. But it could provide succour for congregations at worship, and pastoral care for victims. And so I threw myself into the service of these communities. Outwardly I was confident in my faith, but inwardly I had questions that needed answers.

The first funeral I attended was one I officiated at as a lay pastor. I remember it well for the inner turmoil. A Coloured single mother living in a shack had lost her new-born baby, David. In the pouring rain, a motley crew of Methodists and onlookers filled in the grave at the Grassy Park cemetery with sodden soil while I said the words of the Methodist funeral service: 'It is not the will of your Father which is in heaven, that one of these little ones should perish.' In plain language, doesn't that mean that God does not want innocent children to die? Yet, here I was reading the words of the prayer with which the service ends: 'And now that, in Thine inscrutable wisdom, Thou hast called baby David from our side, help us to trust him to Thy care in the quiet confidence that knows no fear ...'

Why had baby David died? Although I was committed to seeking ordination, this funeral had shaken me. I had bent low to enter the shack in which David's mother lived and had witnessed her poverty and vulnerability. What words of comfort could I give to this heartbroken mother? Can *this* have been an act of God? Did He take the child so he wouldn't grow up in poverty? Or what?

No? Then what meaning can this premature death have? How can such suffering be reconciled with a good and omnipotent God? I found it better to remain silent lest I be guilty of cant and hypocrisy. I was searching for answers ... My questioning extended to the country I lived in.

On 30 March 1960, I was riding my scooter along De Waal Drive when I encountered a large protest march consisting mainly of Africans heading for the city centre. It was a breath-taking sight. Later I was to learn that Philip Kgosana had led the march, consisting of some 30 000 people, in protest at the killings at Sharpeville and Langa. So peaceful was the march that it was reported that not a piece of fruit was stolen from the hawkers' trolleys along the way.

Twenty-two-year-old Kgosana was then a student at the University of Cape Town (UCT) and it fell on his shoulders to lead the march because Robert Sobukwe, leader of the Pan Africanist Congress (PAC), had been jailed. Kgosana led the march in short trousers and a pair of borrowed shoes. Bloodshed was narrowly avoided because of his disciplined hold on the crowd and because of the brave actions of a single police officer, Colonel Terry Terblanche, who defied orders to shoot Kgosana and negotiated with him instead. By agreement, Kgosana handed over a statement and led the march back to the townships.

Later, in a horrific breach of trust, the security police arrested him and he disappeared. The old De Waal Drive is now named after Philip Kgosana in tribute to his great courage, but few if any can remember the names of the authorities who double-crossed him and the crowd he led into Cape Town that fateful day.

How could a system professing Christian values have such scant regard for an agreement forged in such explosive circumstances? Hard to find answers.

It's a disenchanted world

Doubt is the beginning, not the end of wisdom.
– Proverb

'Life can only be understood backwards,' says Søren Kierkegaard, 'but it must be lived forwards.' And it is in the interplay between context and ideas that we gain understanding. I think it's impossible to live without some sort of framework which gives meaning to our lives and helps us to locate ourselves in moral space.

My framework before I went to university to start my theological training was emphatically and uncomplicatedly that of the Christian faith. The world was created by God and entrusted to us to be good stewards of it. Right and wrong were determined by biblical means. God was deeply interested in our personal lives here and beyond the grave. Prayer invoked God's agency when we were confronted with problems and regular worship shaped our day to day behaviour. Such was my taken-for-granted framework.

The Christian faith was for me what the sociologists of knowledge call an exercise in 'world-construction'. Christianity, in other words, made my world.

As I look back, I can see now that my training at Rhodes University in Grahamstown, which began in 1963, turned that world upside down. It was there that I began to understand what I came to call, along with Max Weber, the 'disenchantment of the world'. I was twenty-four years old when I went to Rhodes, a good deal older than the average undergrad, and the first Leatt to attend a university. I took a train to Grahamstown and, as it sped through the Karoo, my excitement grew at the prospect of putting my unexamined Christian faith under the searchlight of scholarship.

The 1960s were exciting and tumultuous times. The expansion of the Vietnam War. The Cuban missile crisis of 1962. John F. Kennedy's assassination in 1963. The advent of the revolutionary birth control pill. Space travel. The hardening of the Cold War. And in South Africa, Sharpeville, the name of a township that was to become the symbol of protest action against the hated pass laws, which restricted the movement of blacks. And the violent response of a repressive regime. UDI in Rhodesia. And, yes, the 'death of God'.

My education began in earnest when I encountered analytical philosophy, which was all the rage when I hit Rhodes. And in 1963, the SCM Press published a cheap edition of *New Essays in Philosophical Theology*, edited by Antony Flew and Alasdair MacIntyre, that introduced me to the problems confronting religious language. In a chapter called 'Theology and Falsification', several university professors famously debated the nature of theological language. Antony Flew blew my mind when he argued that theological assertions, such as 'God loves us like a father loves his children', cannot stand up to the test of falsification. What would count against such an assertion? Can it be falsified? As he said, to know the negation of a statement is, as near as anything, to know the meaning of the statement. But religious people will not allow anything to count against statements like 'God loves us like a father loves his children' or 'God has a plan for your life' or 'God created the world'.

Others entered the debate, some Christians, others not. Basil Mitchell used a parable to illustrate the problem of religious language: It is wartime in an occupied country. A member of the resistance meets a stranger one night. They spend the night together, talking. The Stranger tells the partisan that he himself is on the side of the resistance – indeed, that he is in command of it. He urges the partisan to have faith in him 'no matter what happens'. The partisan is utterly convinced. They never meet one-on-one again.

Sometimes the Stranger is seen helping the resistance. Sometimes he's seen in the uniform of the police, handing over patriots to the occupying power. When this happens his friends begin to murmur against him. But the partisan still says, 'He's on our side.' Despite appearances, the partisan believes the Stranger has not deceived him. The Stranger knows best ... 'Sometimes his friends, in exasperation, say, 'Well, what would he have to do for you to admit that you are wrong and that he is not on our side?' ... 'Well, if that's what you mean by his being on our side, the sooner he goes over to the other side the better.'

What, indeed, would falsify the partisan's claim that the Stranger is on our side? The statement 'God loves us like a father loves his children' and 'The Stranger is on our side' are not conclusively falsifiable. It all depends on the commitment of the one making the claim. The partisan continues to believe despite damning evidence to the contrary. And will continue to do so, I guess, until his experience finally tells against him.

Being a Christian, I could not tolerate that baby David's death of throat cancer, or the death of millions in the Holocaust, should count against the claim 'God loves us like a father loves his children'. To do so would be to question the foundations of my Christian faith. For Jews, Christians or Muslims – monotheists, or anyone who believes in one supreme deity – it's a huge challenge. The *problem of evil* is an age-old conundrum that I wrestled with from the early days of my conversion.

Particularly in my philosophy classes, brilliant teachers encouraged me to question further. It was here that I first discovered the penetrating thought of the eighteenth-century Scottish philosopher, David Hume. Epicurus's old questions from the third century BC are yet unanswered. He wrote: 'Is God willing to prevent evil, but not able? Then he is impotent. Is he able, but not willing? Then he is malevolent. Is he both able and willing? Whence then is evil?'

Religious or theological utterances are intended to provide explanations or express assertions. 'God loves us like a father' looks and feels like an assertion, one that I made Sunday after Sunday from the pulpit and in my pastoral work. Ordinarily, we can say what would count against an assertion. Not so, it seems, when it comes to religious or theological assertions. Back to our parable. Suppose the Stranger is God, says Antony Flew: 'We cannot say that he would like to help but cannot: God is omnipotent. We cannot say that he would help if only he knew: God is omniscient. We cannot say that he is not responsible for the wickedness of others: God creates those others.'

'Death by a thousand qualifications' is how Flew sums up the debate; that is the fate of religious or theological assertions. We say God is all-powerful, but, in the face of the problem of evil, is he? It seems that the religious person is caught on the horns of a dilemma, says Flew. He must engage in what George Orwell called 'doublethink': this is when you hold two contradictory beliefs at the same time, accepting both of them. Telling deliberate lies while believing in them or denying the existence of objective reality while taking account of the reality you deny.

Doublethink is like cognitive dissonance. It's the emotional turmoil you feel when you are trying to hold two inconsistent attitudes or beliefs at the same time, or when there is a conflict between what you believe and how you act. And it illustrates why my foundations at Rhodes began to shake.

The 'scandal of particularity': the phrase belongs to Reinhold Niebuhr. Christianity's claim that 'Jesus is the only way to God' is an example of the scandal of particularity. And it describes a further assault on my unexamined faith. At Rhodes, I read history and social anthropology, in addition to theological subjects. Both disciplines study human history and social formations *comparatively*. The history of religions challenged my cherished belief in the unique claims of the Christian message.

One of my prized books is Mircea Eliade's anthology, *From Primitives to Zen* (1967), which contains key documents from all the main religious traditions except Judaism and Christianity. The readings are arranged according to themes. They include myths of Creation and Origin, the Flood, the Afterlife, the End of the World and Paradise, to name a few. The anthology spans the world of ancient Europe, the Near East, Asia and Africa. It includes the religions of the Celts, the Greeks, Egyptians and Mesopotamians, and covers Hinduism, Jainism, Confucianism, Buddhism and Islam.

Even the succinct summary of moral law given by Jesus – the Golden Rule – can be found in other religious traditions, going back to Confucius, some 2 500 years ago. And so on ... What I thought of as my unassailable, unique Christian faith was simply one belief system alongside others.

Through the discipline of social anthropology I entered the fascinating world of comparative scholarship dedicated to understanding religion, any religion, as a human and social activity. We studied the founding fathers of modern social theory, such as Emile Durkheim (1858–1917) and Max Weber (1864–1920), who were trying to understand the role of religion in the making of the modern world. They took religion seriously and did not try to reduce it to something else or dismiss it as a relic of the premodern world.

I was captivated by Durkheim's view that religion provides the glue that holds societies together. The core values of society are embedded in its espoused religion, he argued. All the more reason to understand the role of religion. Max Weber famously established a link between Protestant Christianity and the rise of modern capitalism. He also made a comparative study of the important role religion played in helping people explain evil and suffering. 'Theodicy' is the word he used to describe the ethical and theological interpretation of pain and suffering in a religious tradition, such as Judaism or Christianity. I'll never forget the sentiments uttered by a Dutch Reformed minister after a mining disaster had claimed a host of lives. He said this was an act of a wrathful God calling a sinful nation to repentance! Why did the miners die? Answer, to bring the nation to its senses. That's theodicy.

It's not difficult to treat such statements with incredulity. But, as

Max Weber argues, at a deeper level, dualism is a type of theodicy that pits the forces of truth and light against the powers of falsehood and darkness. Zoroastrianism, still practised by Parsees today, teaches this form of dualism. Good and evil are seen as radically opposing forces locked in an eternal battle. God's creation is good, with evil trying to destroy it. A less consistent form can be found in religious traditions that speak of heaven and hell, of God's triumph over the forces of evil and of a saviour's triumph over the devil.

The point about such social theories was that they revealed family traits in religions as different as Confucianism, Judaism, Christianity, Islam and African indigenous religions. They all played a role in the cohesion of societies that practised them and provided explanations for bad times when people suffered. Comparatively speaking, what I had been saying as a lay pastor to Christian congregations Sunday after Sunday was simply not *literally* true. What Christianity offered was *not* unique as it was offered in a different voice by other religious traditions, using different metaphors.

What to make of all this? While I entered into this fascinating world of scholarship, I still followed the discipline of the Church. However, I was becoming increasingly uncomfortable with the claim that belief in Jesus Christ was the *only* road to salvation. Methodism is part of the evangelical tradition within Christianity, and, as a Methodist, I believed that Jesus was *the* way to God, and preached it. At Rhodes, my 'evangelical Christianity' encountered Niebuhr's 'scandal of particularity'.

The comparative study of religious beliefs and practices opened my eyes to the extraordinary diversity of religions and enabled me to see the stories they shared. Joseph Campbell was fond of saying that every religion is 'true' when understood metaphorically. But you get into trouble when you interpret metaphors as facts.

When I was at Rhodes, candidates for the ministry of the Anglican, Methodist, Congregational and Presbyterian churches were given lectures on what is called 'Apologetics' – the defence of the faith. Some of us were beginning to ask: is there a reality to which the word 'religion' points? We spent hours inside and outside the classroom debating the powerful critiques of religion mounted by those two giants of the modern world, Karl Marx and Sigmund Freud.

Karl Marx (1818–1883), who died just a few years before my father was born, argued that 'the criticism of religion is the premise of all criticism'. And he thought that, by the mid-nineteenth century, the task had mostly been accomplished, and it was time to move on to politics! This is how he saw the critique of religion:

> The abolition of religion as the *illusory* happiness of the people is the demand for their *real* happiness. The demand to abandon illusions about their real conditions is a *demand to abandon a condition which requires illusions*. The criticism of religion is thus the *germ* of the *criticism of the vale of tears* of which religion is the *halo*.

Marx famously went on to say that criticism is not enough; the point is to *change* society. Religion alienates people because it encourages them to accept their servitude as workers on the promise of life beyond the grave, where the tables will be turned on the capitalist owners of the means of production. For Marx, religion was an ideology rooted in the material conditions of life; as such, it masked what was really going on and therefore needed to be abolished.

Sigmund Freud (1856–1939), who died in the year that I was born, pioneered a psychological critique of religion as a projection of repressed desires. Psychoanalysis, according to Freud, argues that a personal God is nothing other than an exalted father, a projection. Young people lose their religious beliefs as soon as they break with their father's authority.

When I reflected on Freud's critique of religion as projection, I could see that in my teens I had found comfort in a personal God who watched over me. In his 1927 book, *The Future of an Illusion*, Freud argues that religious beliefs are not just an expression of people's wishes and fears; they are a compensation for life's vagaries. Wouldn't it be nice if there were a god, who was both creator of the world and a benevolent providence? Wouldn't it be nice if there were a moral order and an afterlife? But, says Freud, it is a 'very striking fact that this is exactly as we are bound to wish it to be.' And so he concludes that 'the religions of mankind must be classed among the mass-delusions'!

My grappling with these intellectual challenges helped me to develop what C. Wright Mills called a 'sociological imagination'. This is the ability to see the role and function of such institutions as marriage, rites of passage, even religion. Marriage, it seems, takes many forms and is universal, enabling societies to control adult sexual behaviour and ensure the reproduction of the species. Religion enables an individual to identify with the group, supports her in her uncertainty, provides consolation when she is troubled, schools her in society's goals, boosts her morale, and so on. Religion, it seems, is a cultural universal. We know of no society that totally lacks the cultural patterns that we can refer to as religious. Regardless of creed, religion fulfils these and similar functions in society. This does not mean, of course, that all people in all societies over time are, in any meaningful sense, religious.

It was Max Weber who first drew my attention to the 'de-sacralising' of the world and its consequences. One of the founding fathers of modern sociology, Weber argued that the making of the modern world depended on what he called 'rationalisation'. This progressive 'disenchantment of the world' eliminated supernatural or magical thought and practice. What is science but the *rationalisation of nature*? Once you grasp that the world works according to the laws of nature and not according to the vagaries of magic or the whims of the gods, science and technology become possible. In *Looking in the Distance* (2004), Richard Holloway captures the gist of the idea of, disenchantment as follows:

> Traditional religions have a picture of God as a superhuman person, possessing absolute power over us, who inhabits a heavenly realm that is separated from the earth, but is in regular contact with it, the way NASA communicates with its space stations. Many people find the NASA model for God, as a supernatural engineering and maintenance agency, very difficult to hold today.

But we should not confuse disenchantment with the end of religion. It's just that this secularity has made it more and more difficult to believe in a NASA-like God or the idea of the supernatural acting on the world.

It was Weber who helped me to understand the meaning of modernity. I know 'modernity' is a contested notion, but an alien visitor to this planet would notice that the key marker of modernity is our technological ability to alter nature to suit our ends. This power over matter, over life on the planet, and over humankind itself, grows exponentially. And the exercise of this power over two centuries has done much to improve the quality of life in the world as never before. Not even the ravages of two world wars – themselves examples of our advanced technological prowess – could stem the tide.

In short, the 'rationalisation' of nature through science has fundamentally altered the human condition. Abraham of the Bible and my paternal great-great-great grandfather probably had much in common; neither would feel at home in my world, and I have little in common with theirs.

Weber went further. Bureaucracy is nothing else but the 'rationalisation of the collective'. Neither the modern state nor the

23

modern business enterprise could operate without bureaucracy. It is rationally calculable principles that make the modern business organisation or public administration. Indeed, modern capitalism itself is premised on the idea that productivity and profitability are rational ends.

We may sometimes curse civil servants, and bewail our feeling trapped in one or another organisation, but we could not run modern society without bureaucracy. What distinguishes modern society is the *calculus* of systems and combinations of skills and technologies needed to administer something efficiently and effectively. Without these systems, you can't apply for a driver's licence or bank loan, reserve seats in the cinema, or replenish the shelves in the retail store.

In the1960s, two philosophers of science held a public debate in London. At stake was how to understand the role of science in the modern world.

They were the famous Karl Popper (1902–1994) and the younger, up-and-coming Thomas Kuhn (1922–1996). Kuhn had recently published *The Structure of Scientific Revolutions* (1962), which became, arguably, the most influential book on the nature of science in the twentieth century. Popper was known worldwide for his work on the nature of 'open', as opposed to 'closed', societies, for his work on the logic of scientific discovery and for his famous principle of 'falsifiability'. He was knighted in 1965.

Kuhn argued that working scientists accept the dominant scientific 'paradigm' (a word Kuhn made famous) of the day and get on with their 'normal' science. They are reluctant to jettison the paradigm and are ill-equipped to consider fundamental changes in research direction.

He thought the scientific community behaved much like a religious order. And he defended science's autonomy against political, economic or social regulation in the period of the Cold War. Within the closed community of scientists, paradigms are shared and behaviour is self-regulated. Scientific revolutions are few and far between and they succeed because different views gain traction when a new breed of scientist adopts a new paradigm. The paradigm shift that occurs in a scientific revolution is much like a religious conversion. Truth is to be found in the beliefs and actions of the community of scientists who hold them to be true.

For centuries, people believed the Earth was the centre of the universe. It was called the Ptolemaic or geometric system. Only when the Catholic astronomer and mathematician Copernicus provided a mathematical model for a heliocentric universe did that paradigm change. The Copernican revolution has the Earth and planets revolving around a relatively stationary sun.

Popper, whom I'd read at Rhodes, wanted to know what would count for any citizen as evidence against *any* truth claim. Knowledge claims, including scientific claims, should be accountable to a public procedure that tests such claims. How else are we to protect ourselves against the rise of totalitarian regimes, especially if such claims come from a political party or leader?

Popper formulated his 'falsifiability principle' to test the claims of any belief, scientific or not. This took me back to my student days. Theological and scientific hypotheses must face the tribunal of experimental experience. If a hypothesis survives this ordeal, it can be provisionally accepted as corroborated, until such time as something occurs that calls it into question; yes, that falsifies it.

Science proceeds by 'conjectures' (hypotheses) and 'refutations'; it is *in principle*, then, an *open* process. As Steve Fuller says, Popper's philosophy of science and his democratic philosophy are *both* expressions of what he called 'the open society'. No elite, not even a community of scientists, is immune from the principle of falsifiability, whereby their ideas and actions can be tested and, if necessary, refuted. Any society that protects an elite group, be they scientists or not, from such scrutiny is at risk of becoming what Popper called a 'closed society'.

The overriding metaphors that shape the world we live in come from science and technology. We are accustomed to thinking of myths as the opposite of science. In common language, to say something is a myth is to say that it is a lie. Yet, myth can embrace a larger meaning as a product of the imagination, a powerful set of symbols that suggest a way of interpreting the world.

When we say the laws of nature are like clockwork, or when we use the image of the machine to describe the regularity of nature, or of the computer to describe the brain, or speak of genetic engineering, or the building blocks of life, we are using powerful metaphors, even symbol systems – yes, even myths. They are the dominant 'reality-generating mechanisms' of our time. Science is a source of *values* – some would say the only true source of them. Mary Midgley is right: we don't need to tell each other that science is good any more than we need to say that freedom is good or democracy is good.

But science is not omnicompetent. It's not the source of values, and its progress is neither inevitable nor necessarily good. To believe any of this is to fall into the trap of scientism, the view that 'there is no question whose answer is in principle unattainable by science'. How do you test this claim? What would count against it? The claim is an act of faith for which we have no proof.

Well, when I left Rhodes in 1965, my Christian faith was bloodied but as yet unbowed. How did I hold it together? I knew that few are gifted with a faith that is free of doubt. I was embarking on a career. And had a lot to offer. I had spent six long years preparing for this. So, I allowed myself to be carried along by the institutional imperatives of the Methodist Church.

Fortunately, *Speaking of God* by William Horden came into my hands about this time. Like me, Horden had had his faith shaken by analytical philosophy. Taking his cue from Ludwig Wittgenstein's writings, he found a way to speak of God that helped me at the time. The Austrian-born Wittgenstein (1889–1951), who taught philosophy at Cambridge, was by all accounts an eccentric, troubled genius. He observed how language works when it is 'idling' and noticed that we use a variety of what he calls 'language games', each with their own 'rules'. The rules we use in daily life for determining what is 'good', what is 'true' and what is 'beautiful' are different, and we get into all sorts of muddles when we confuse them. Science uses the language of empirical observation and falsification to assert that something is 'true'. The language game of aesthetics uses different rules for demonstrating the truth of a claim such as 'Leonardo da Vinci's *Mona Lisa* is a masterpiece.' And we use different rules, again, when we want to make moral claims about what is 'good', or about what we ought to do.

Horden examines the language game of theology. How does it work, and what are the rules? He points out that when Jews or Christians or Muslims speak of God they're not making scientific statements. Insiders, religious people, use analogy, symbol and metaphor. They usually speak from a community of faith, from the heart, with conviction. They use words like 'transcendent', and speak of the mystery of God, meaning that the more they explore the mystery the more profound it is.

At the time, the analogy of language games gave me a way of speaking meaningfully of God. The biblical myth of creation is not competing with the theory of evolution; it is making a statement about the worth or dignity of the natural world. Since I could not bring myself to believe in the bodily resurrection and ascension of Jesus, I could demythologise these doctrines; Jesus lives on in his church. Rudolf Bultmann, a German theologian best known for his attempts to demythologise religion, argued that the myths of the past should not be treated as pseudo-scientific or even pre-scientific statements. They were attempts to speak of God in the only language known at the time. And it is not difficult to understand what they were attempting to say, given modern hermeneutics – the art of interpreting texts.

Interlude

Simon's Town, 1966 – my first appointment as an ordained minister. Four years earlier, I met Jenny at a Methodist youth camp. She lived in Cape Town and I was a probation minister in Bellville. We fell in love and became engaged when Jenny turned twenty-one. A long courtship followed as I had to complete the year at Bellville before reading for my degree at Rhodes University.

The Methodist rule at the time was that probationers could not marry until their university training was done. And I didn't have the gumption to disobey the rule, as Leslie Weatherhead had in England. When he was hauled before a disciplinary committee to explain himself, he apologised profusely and promised not to do it again. Jenny and I were married soon after my ordination in 1965.

The manse in Simon's Town, quaintly called the 'Methodist Parsonage', was our first home, a Victorian house situated on the slope of the mountain above the harbour. I can still hear the sea lapping against the boats below us, and recall the long passage covered with black linoleum, with the loo at the end of it.

I threw myself into the issues of the day. A year later, the Christian Institute (CI), founded by Beyers Naudé, awarded me a travelling fellowship, which enabled Jenny and I to venture beyond South Africa for three months – our first overseas visit.

I suppose it was a sign of my increasing sense of alienation that I chose not to look at core Church activities but rather at the Church's attempts in Europe to bridge the gap between itself and the industrial society – the 'industrial mission', as it was called in those days. Here I was drawing on my Methodist roots. John and Charles Wesley had a profound impact on the making of the English working class and the process of industrialisation in Britain. I also chose to look at the role the Lutheran Church played in the reconstruction of Germany after the Second World War – the Lay Academy Movement.

One of the objectives of the CI fellowship was to allow the recipient to gain perspective on our troubled land. Apartheid, the legalisation of racism, was not that old, but already South Africa was becoming a pariah nation in the eyes of the world. Now, we could view our country from afar.

Jenny and I visited industrial missions in the north of England and in Germany, as well as a Protestant monastery in Taizé, France. Industrial mission clergy took leave of absence from their churches to work in factories, joined trade unions and experienced industrial capitalism at the coalface. The levels of alienation from the church in the UK and in Germany were vast. In one place we were told of workers who thought Grace was a girl's name. They had no inkling of the Christian doctrine of giving thanks before meals.

In Germany, church attendance had plummeted but the lay academies were strong. Essentially, they were church-sponsored residential conference centres for people from different walks of life to get together to reconstruct their professions and vocations and figure out how to contribute to the rebuilding of Germany. The question the Protestant Church was asking itself was, 'How did it come about that after preaching the pure reformed gospel for four hundred years there could arise a Hitler and a Third Reich?'

Simon's Town had been racially mixed for as long as anyone could remember. The town was named after Simon van der Stel who had carried out a survey of False Bay in 1687 for the Dutch East India Company. It became the port for the Company in 1743. Centuries of intermarriage and social interaction made it a culturally diverse community, whose history and heritage were probably unique in South Africa.

When we arrived in 1966, the effects of various apartheid laws were already being felt. The Immorality Act outlawed courting across the colour line. The Mixed Marriages Act outlawed racial intermarriage. Blood sisters had to visit racially segregated prenatal clinics – one for white pregnant mothers, the other for Coloured mothers.

But it was the dreaded Group Areas Act that was to change Simon's Town profoundly. During our brief tenure, desperate attempts were made to seek a stay of execution and make Simon's Town an exception. The churches and civil society rallied to the cause. But, sadly, all these efforts failed and the guillotine fell on 1 September 1967. The whole of the municipal area of Simon's Town was declared a Group Area for Whites only. Everyone who was not classified White became a disqualified person scheduled to be moved out of the area at the stroke of a pen. Racially mixed families would meet around the grave of a deceased family member but could not live together.

Amid busy-ness, I postponed reflection on whether or not I really belonged in the ministry at all. James, the social worker and an activist with a dog collar, engaged in his own, local version of industrial mission. Added to which I had registered to read for the BA Honours in Social Anthropology at UCT. The field work involved a study of a Coloured community living in Red Hill above Simon's Town, all of whom were affected by the Group Areas Act.

After two eventful years in Simon's Town, we were appointed to the Inner City Mission (ICM) headquartered in District Six in Cape Town and served mainly the Coloured community, as far afield as Darling, forty kilometres away up the West Coast. Peter Storey was the ICM superintendent. And it was here, in a small house in Claremont, rented by the Church, that our son, Christopher, was born in 1968. Two years later we were on the move again, to the manse in Mowbray, where our daughter, Ann-Marie, was born in 1970. Apparently, I hadn't escaped my itinerant past. It was in the ICM that Jenny and I learned by trial and error to cope with early parenthood.

The work of the ICM was just as challenging. Everywhere you looked the apartheid apparatus was destroying communities with historic roots in the city and environs. The ICM was actively involved in trying to stop this, and developed imaginative programmes to build a community, at least within the church. Members of the congregation self-built a multipurpose church and hall in Nuwedorp, Darling. We built an early-learning centre, one of the first, in Windermere (now Kensington). We developed the Carpenter's House for the youth of District Six, where forced removals were 'relocating' thousands of people to the sprawling townships on the Cape Flats. We ran a weekly My Brother and Me programme, designed to address racism and build racial tolerance. Today the church in Buitenkant Street, District Six, is part of the District Six Museum.

Despite my work with the ICM, I wanted to continue my studies. In 1970, when UCT established a Department of Religious Studies, I registered for my doctorate. Here, I discovered a kindred spirit in Professor John Cumpsty, who had just been appointed as the first head of the new department. Like me, he had a lifelong interest in Reinhold Niebuhr (1892–1971). So I chose as my topic the life and thought of Niebuhr.

In the preface to my doctoral dissertation I wrote: 'Niebuhr is widely acknowledged as the most influential Christian social ethicist of the twentieth century. What attracted me was that for over fifty years he grappled with the issues which confronted his native America at a time when that nation was undergoing the most dramatic change in its history as it took on the mantle of world leadership.'

In all his years of teaching at the famous Union Theological Seminary in New York, Niebuhr refused the title of theologian, although his formal writing in theology was extensive and influential. He preferred to be known as a Christian ethicist or moral philosopher with a pragmatic bent. Towards the end of his long career, he often expressed regret that political leaders frequently agreed with his moral stance even when they could not agree with its roots in Protestant Christianity.

Niebuhr wrote many books and journal articles, and he was a

public intellectual of some standing, writing perceptively about contemporary dilemmas. I could understand what he was saying. His ethics derived from his Protestant Christianity, the very tenets many of his peers could no longer accept. I too found that I no longer got excited about the theological tenets of Protestantism, but I admired Niebuhr's grappling with the ethical issues of his time. What happens when you can no longer accept the tenets upon which your ethics is based? What would a secular ethics look like? These questions were to come sharply into focus.

The Methodist Church sent the newly capped 'Dr' Leatt to teach at the Federal Theological Seminary (Fedsem) in Alice, in what is now the Eastern Cape. This is where the Anglican, Methodist, Congregational and Presbyterian churches trained their black ministers. It was here that I developed a love for teaching. There was nothing quite like the thrill of the classroom, or the informal discussions in our lounge at the seminary. I felt privileged to be part of the process.

And to meet people like Walter Mbete. He was an ex-gangster from Port Elizabeth who came to Fedsem as a trainee for the Methodist ministry. He was a keen student who quickly made up the deficits in his education and thrived in this environment. Later he went into voluntary exile to be a chaplain of the ANC's Umkhonto we Sizwe (MK) cadres.

As a family, we loved Alice. We were part of a non-racial community – a rarity in South Africa at the time. We loved our college house, and soon after we arrived invited the staff of John Wesley College to tea. We'd hung a picture on the wall above the fireplace. It was an Arthur English colour photograph of Table Mountain taken from Bloubergstrand, with Robben Island in the foreground. Simon Gqubule, the Principal, looked at it and said, 'When I stood on the slopes of Table Mountain and looked at Robben Island, I wept.' Quick as a flash, Stanley Mogoba, a lecturer, who had been a political prisoner on Robben Island, said, 'And when I stood on Robben Island and looked at Table Mountain, I wept.'

I found the change from pastoral work invigorating. I was paid a stipend to think and to teach. What a pleasure! The Fedsem library was well stocked and I relished the opportunity to read.

Alice is in a part of the Eastern Cape that was steeped in educational innovation through institutions like the Lovedale College and the University of Fort Hare. Christopher and Ann-Marie loved seminary life. They had wide open spaces in which to play with the children of staff and students of the seminary. At a time when black and white South Africans rarely mixed, they formed friendships with black children and experienced the comings and goings of a thoroughly multiracial community. When we took our children to see the Lipizzaner horses on display near Cape Town during a holiday, Ann-Marie seemed troubled. 'Where are the people?' she asked. It was her first conscious registering of segregation in South Africa.

Established in 1963 with funding support from the International Missionary Council and the Christian Council of South Africa, Fedsem was a symbol of ecumenism and a thorn in the side of the apartheid regime. It was a beautifully designed, custom-built campus for about a hundred students plus staff – a community of some one hundred and fifty people.

Fedsem was often blamed for causing all the trouble at the University of Fort Hare, its close neighbour. Disaster struck a year into our idyllic stay at Fedsem. On 26 November 1974, in a misguided attempt to silence protesting students at Fort Hare, Fedsem was served with a notice of expropriation. The document, signed by Hendrik Schoeman, the Minister of Agriculture, gave the seminary thirty days to vacate the property. The government used an obscure piece of legislation to expropriate the land and buildings of the seminary. On 27 December 1974, the land and buildings of the seminary would be transferred to the South African Bantu Trust and thereafter be made available to the University of Fort Hare.

Government seemed to be under the misapprehension that our students were the cause of the ongoing student unrest at Fort Hare. However, we knew our older students were a moderating influence.

The Governing Council of the seminary had been dealing with pressure and unwarranted interference from the Rector of Fort Hare since at least 1971, when the university had offered to purchase Fedsem. But the expropriation order came as a shock. Government turned a deaf ear to the submissions of the Council and the churches. Even pleas for a stay of execution and time to find an alternative site failed. The Council finally resolved to relocate to St Bede's College in Umtata (now Mthatha).

We built a temporary campus there. Just two weeks after the installation of the seminary in Umtata, a group of Fedsem students organised a Black Heroes' Day service at a Presbyterian church in Ngangeliswe, near St Bede's. Informers present gave an alarming report to the cabinet of the Transkeian government. Chief Minister Kaiser Matanzima railed against Fedsem and threatened to expropriate all Anglican land in Transkei.

The conflict between Fedsem and the Transkeian government spilled over to St Bede's and involved the local Anglican bishop. Despite the Fedsem Council trying to mend the fences, Fedsem was ordered to leave St Bede's. A temporary home was found at the Lay Ecumenical Centre at Edendale in then Natal, while a new seminary was built on land at Imbali nearby. The seminary moved to its new temporary home on 11 December 1975.

After much agonising, Jenny and I left the seminary at that point. Our two children were now in their third school in as many years. I did not want my children to relive my nomadic early schooling. With great sadness, I asked for leave of absence from the Church and we moved back to Cape Town. Jobless.

So, when in 1976, the Dean of Cape Town, Ted King, asked me to be part of an experimental ministry at St George's Cathedral, called simply The Centre, I jumped at it. We had no home and little furniture, having lived in furnished manses all our married life. With a generous interest-free loan from my uncle, we set about finding our first family home. Pinelands was an ideal suburb for young children; they could walk or ride their bicycles everywhere. There was a lively babysitting circle. Our house was just right for our young family. It needed attention but it was *our* home and we spent a very happy decade there.

The Cathedral was attempting to bridge the gap between the Church and the city. One part of the experiment involved the creative arts. My part was a form of industrial mission, called the Urban Ministries Project. John Cumpsty and I developed a background paper on urban ministry, which informed my work. We argued that urban ministry is ministry to society. It is a half of the Church's ministry if the other half is to individuals.

These were tense times. The Soweto uprising began on 16 June 1976. Sixteen years after Sharpeville, anger against apartheid once again led to nationwide protests, this time led by schoolchildren who were refusing the use of Afrikaans as a medium of instruction for key subjects. The violent state response left 176 people dead. The Centre was hosting a Ministry in Our Cities consultation around this time that was disrupted because of the teargas used by the police to break up protests in Cape Town.

I wrote a paper for the consultation, called 'The Church's Care of Society', drawing on the work John Cumpsty and I had done. I argued that a healthy society operated out of a fellowship of agreed principles about where it wanted to go. The church's care of society includes a ministry to men and women in responsibility whose decisions, piece by piece, construct the kind of society we live in. Later, I drew on these experiences in a business school context.

The experimental Centre at the Cathedral depended on donor funding. My job was precarious. I needed something more permanent, ideally a teaching job at a university. That's what I wanted.

Imagine my delight when, in 1977, I was appointed as a lecturer in the Department of Religious Studies at UCT.

While at UCT, I finally resigned from the Methodist Church. I felt estranged, no longer one of the clergy, and out of sync with the Church. In my letter of resignation I expressed my gratitude for the education the Church had given me. But I said that it would be difficult for me to subject myself to the doctrines and disciplines of the Methodist Church in my secular job.

The Methodist Church had been my home and my haven for some twenty years. Cutting my ties was a major signpost on my journey. Memory is mutable, a fickle thing, but, looking back, I had over time ceased to be a practising Christian. Our 'odyssey of soul runs in counterpoint to our odyssey of life', says Thomas Moore.

I like the way Moore talks about the soul as that which holds together mind and body, ideas and life, spirituality and life. Certainly, what was going on in my life was running parallel and at a different pace to what was happening in my soul. I felt something new stirring in me, something yet to be born. Moore quotes the poet Wallace Stevens: 'What was the purpose of his pilgrimage? To make a new intelligence prevail.' Now I had to make my way in the secular world.

Hard at work, teaching back to back in popular undergraduate courses in an under-resourced department, I was stretched and stressed, but I loved it. And I was also beginning to develop research interests. Yet, I was unprepared for the turn of events that was to redraw the map.

Desmond Tutu, then General Secretary of the South African Council of Churches (SACC), offered to mediate in an ongoing industrial relations dispute – a strike that involved Fatti's & Moni's, a leading pasta-making company, and an unregistered, illegal trade union. Both parties to the dispute were hurting. The company faced the threat of a national boycott of its products, while the workers had been on strike for some six months. To everyone's great surprise, both the union and management accepted his offer. The SACC was now looking for someone to mediate in the dispute.

I received a call out of the blue from Peter Storey on behalf of the SACC. 'Can you assist?' Peter and I had worked together before, and he had been instrumental in getting me stationed in the Inner City Mission when he was its superintendent. Why did they call me? I can only assume that it was because Peter knew of my interest in industrial mission. I knew little about industrial disputes, but the SACC would not take no for an answer. So I agreed.

I quickly learned that mediation between an 'unregistered' (not legally recognised) trade union and a company had not been tried before. The mediation was all the more difficult because of the nationwide community support the workers enjoyed. There were actually three parties to the mediation: the pasta company, the trade union, and the community organisations supporting a boycott of company products. The strike was deemed illegal and the normal industrial relations processes didn't apply. Where to start? I talked to labour economists and to colleagues at UCT's Graduate School of Business (GSB). I met with management and with union leaders. 'Don't negotiate positions,' I was advised, 'always seek to negotiate interests.' Well, Fatti's & Moni's feared a national boycott of its products and was willing to compromise, while the striking members of the African Food and Canning Workers' Union had been without wages for six months. It was in the interests of both parties to find a way forward. I recall the tension in the room when management had to come to terms with the cost of settling versus the risk of a boycott. As a third party in this mediation, I could see the ground on which both parties could stand if they wanted to settle.

Finally, after shuttle diplomacy and a great deal of help, we found a way to resolve the dispute and enable the workers to return to work with improved wages and benefits. One of the complications was the company's employment of scab labour. Any settlement had to involve their retrenchment on terms that were fair.

38

I wrote up the case, which was published in several journals, and I was party to the launching of a national independent mediation service, a precursor to today's Commission for Conciliation, Mediation and Arbitration (CCMA).

In the early 1980s, the gold mining industry was wracked by outbreaks of what was popularly called 'faction fighting' – violent clashes between groups of migrant miners that often left a trail of bloodshed and death. In a historic and unprecedented move, the Anglo American Corporation, in the person of its then Director of Industrial Relations, Bobby Godsell, and the National Union of Mineworkers (NUM), in the person of its General Secretary, Cyril Ramaphosa, decided to investigate.

I was asked, together with Paulus Zulu, to lead the investigation. Godsell and Ramaphosa would jointly chair a steering committee made up of Anglo and NUM representatives. Conventional wisdom held that ethnicity was the root cause of the violence. How could we test this? Paulus and I visited Anglo mines, donned helmets, went down shafts, visited migrant hostels and witnessed the induction programme that acclimatised miners for the severe conditions thousands of metres underground. We designed a massive inquiry, conducted by mining and union staff jointly, that finally led to a substantial report, published in May 1986: *Reaping the Whirlwind*.

What we found turned conventional wisdom on its head. The prevailing view was that mine violence is ethnic – such as Xhosa-speaking miners from the Eastern Cape fighting with Sesotho-speakers from Lesotho. Our research revealed something different. Let's say a fight broke out in a shebeen over a prostitute. If it escalated, the Xhosa miner would look for support from men from his home region and the miner from Lesotho would do the same. At base, mine violence usually occurred when conflict over resources like jobs, housing, places in schools, and the like escalated into what appeared to be an ethnic conflict. In reality, faction fighting was, and is, actually conflict over scarce resources. Given today's concerns about xenophobia, I believe this research is still of relevance. The report represented a large-scale effort at social problem solving. Again, the context was a troubled period in South Africa, exemplified by the NUM's discovery of teargas ducts in Anglo mines designed to quell mine violence – a discovery that threatened to put an end to NUM/Anglo cooperation in the mine violence investigation.

Today, with the large numbers of immigrants in our major cities, it is not surprising that South Africa experiences sporadic outburst of violent xenophobia. In a sense, South Africa today can be said to be the mining context of the 1980s writ large. And the lessons of *Reaping the Whirlwind* still apply. When competition for scarce resources leads to violence, the root cause is not ethnicity but scarcity.

Secular sources of meaning

The universe is under no obligation to make
sense to you.
– Neil deGrasse Tyson

Over the course of time the seeds of doubt sewn during my years at Rhodes grew. I slowly began to take on board, first with my head and then with my heart, the notion of the 'disenchantment of the world'. And, like many before me, I began to understand that the worldview of the early Christians and mine were poles apart – fundamentally different.

And I found myself on a journey in search of secular sources of meaning and of The Self. If we can no longer look to the supernatural for the meaning of the cosmos, where do we look? If I no longer can believe in the providential hand of God in human affairs, what is the purpose of my life? Whence our sense of right and wrong? Of the Good? And what about our self-understanding? Without God and the support of organised religion, how are we to make sense of ourselves and our place in the modern world?

Weber called it 'disenchantment', Nietzsche spoke of 'the death of God'. Dostoevsky had one of his characters saying, 'If God does not exist, everything is permitted'. These striking ideas highlight something that is unique in the experience of humankind. Our *loss* of the divine sense of the cosmos as a meaningful order. Few of us believe any longer that 'God is in heaven and all's right with the world'. Modernity means we live in a world where science has closed the gaps in our understanding of our reality. It has become the dominant motif. As science has diminished the gaps in our knowledge, we no longer believe in what Dietrich Bonhoeffer famously called a 'God of the gaps'.

Increasing numbers of people no longer look to the supernatural to fathom the world or our place in it.

But surely science as science cannot be our *source* of meaning? As Ludwig Wittgenstein famously put it: 'We feel that even when *all possible* scientific questions have been answered, the problems of life remain completely untouched.'

Where then, or how, are we to find meaning? How do we escape meaninglessness? Confronted by these existential questions, I turned to the tools of sociology and of moral philosophy for help.

Let us put our sociological imaginations to work and explore the interplay between history, society and biography. Enter Peter Berger, one of the leading proponents of what is called the sociology of knowledge. I first met Berger in print in the 1960s when he published an influential book on the sociology of religion, *The Sacred Canopy: Elements of a Sociological Theory of Religion* (1967). We are all engaged, he says, in the social construction of reality. 'Every human society is an enterprise of world-building'. I met him in person in the 1980s as part of the South Africa beyond Apartheid project of which he was the research director.

There is a profound sense, says Berger, in which society is a product of humankind. And, the opposite is true also; I am a product of society: We are born into a socially constructed world and we have to fashion a meaningful place for ourselves in it. In a sense, then, it's an 'open' world into which we are born. And we must 'make' a world for ourselves – engage continuously in 'world construction'. How does this work? Well, we are born into a world that existed before us and will remain after we've departed. Hopefully, we may have left it a little better for our being here. In other words, the world is 'external' to us. In the process of growing up and becoming socialised, we 'internalise' the world and it begins to take on a certain 'objectivity'. As though it is 'out there' in some sense. It begins to possess a kind of 'taken-for-granted' quality for us.

If you were a male born into the social class of landed gentry in the England of the sixteenth century, your social world would have been hierarchical and you would have been expected to take your place as rentier living off the land. Your family might have even endowed the church you attend and almost certainly you would have believed in God as portrayed by the Anglican Church. History and biography would have intersected in this taken-for-granted world of yours to give you a sense of meaning and moral space.

Now, the thing about a taken-for-granted world is that it appears to operate quietly in the background without us really noticing that it is there. It's only when we come up against something in our personal or collective lives that challenges this world that we become conscious of it. For our young member of the landed gentry what came to be known as the Protestant Reformation would have almost certainly turned his taken-for-granted world upside down.

This brings us to another feature of this process of world-construction. The social world of our young member of the landed gentry takes on an objective and subjective reality for him. What the sociologists call a 'nomos', a Greek word meaning law or custom. The things he believes and the way he behaves have a normative quality about them. This *is* the way the world is. Language, theories about the world, religious beliefs and practices, ways of understanding right from wrong, ways of relating to members of your class and those beneath your class all contrive to establish this *nomos*.

But, as Berger points out, all socially constructed worlds are 'inherently precarious'. In the ordinary course of things our taken-for-granted worlds are supported and confirmed – 'legitimated', as the sociologists say. In other words, when 'why' questions arise there are mechanisms to underpin the taken-for-granted. If these mechanisms fail for some reason the questioner experiences a sense of 'alienation'.

What could go wrong? Well, our young member of the landed gentry might fall in love with a woman below his social class and be faced with a cruel existential choice. Either he loses the love of his life or he risks the wrath of his parents, even of being disinherited.

That could shake his foundations and cause him to feel alienated from his class. Suddenly all the things that seemed *plausible* are called into question. The world he knows begins to totter, and his subjective certainties are called into question. He feels alienated, out of sorts with his world.

Throughout human history, religion has played a decisive part in the enterprise of world construction. Using our sociological imaginations we can see how this works. For much of human history that socially constructed *nomos* we have been talking about was profoundly religious. Religion can be understood as the human enterprise 'by which a sacred cosmos is established', says Peter Berger. Put differently, religion is the daring endeavour on the part of humankind to imagine the universe as humanly significant. For many, it is *the* source of meaning.

And for much of human history the world was 'enchanted'. The king ruled by divine decree, the chief played a sacred role in the tribe, the river was not only a source of life, it was sacred. Rain came and crops grew because the spirits were placated. Status was ascribed by your God-given place in the world and not achieved by your own efforts. 'The rich man in his castle/the poor man at his gate' – each had their 'appointed' place in the scheme of things. Religion was, to use Berger's graphic metaphor, a 'sacred canopy' under which the drama of ordinary life was played.

Power can reside in things. Things external to us. Spirits, demons, and the like. 'In fact, in the enchanted world, the line between personal agency and impersonal force was not at all clearly drawn', says the Canadian philosopher of note, Charles Taylor; the human being was 'porous' (*A Secular Age*, 2007). This powerful metaphor helped me get a sense of what it means to live in an enchanted world. Porousness means being vulnerable to outside forces. Take the fear of possession. Demons can possess you and cause you grief. Indeed, in an enchanted world mental illness was laid at the door of possession. For the porous self is wide-open to spirits, demons, and cosmic forces. With porousness comes vulnerability to the external and ubiquitous world of the supernatural. And with this vulnerability comes the need to propitiate, to take action to buy or win the favour of these forces.

Consider how melancholy would be viewed in an enchanted world. If you are feeling melancholy or depressed, you would be considered to have a case of black bile. But black bile is not the cause of melancholy it *embodies* it, it *is* melancholy. And you won't recover until it has been purged from your body. Contrast this with our modern, disenchanted view of depression which affects millions of people. Today, few people would attribute it to black bile or the work of malevolent spirits.

Porousness. This is the way the world is experienced by those for whom the world is not disenchanted. So, whether I'm a Thai villager in Bangkok, or a Xhosa herdsman in the Easter Cape, or a devout Southern Baptist in the USA, or a pious Jew in Jerusalem, or a staunch member of the African Independent Zionist Christian Church, or a practising Catholic in Barcelona, I am beholden to extra-human sources of power. For good or evil. Planting a crop, choosing a life partner, feuding with a neighbour are ventures fraught with risk. I need cosmic goodwill on my side.

In an enchanted world, I am open, porous and vulnerable to the supernatural. Disbelief is difficult. I take refuge under the sacred canopy. As Charles Taylor says, it's virtually impossible not to believe in the agency of the sacred in some form.

A sociologist might attempt an answer to Taylor this way: it's hard to believe in God today because the plausibility of the 'sacred canopy' of religion has been undermined, weakened by secular modernity. Modernity in the form of the historical processes that gave rise to the capitalist economy, industrialisation (including the Fourth Industrial Revolution), science and technology. In times past, questions about meaning and ethics were resolved within the sanctuary provided by the 'sacred canopy'. Not so today. Secularisation has brought about a 'demonopolisation' of religious traditions says Peter Berger; it represents a severe 'rupture' of the traditional task of religion, which was precisely the establishment of a cohesive set of definitions of reality that could serve as a common universe of meaning for members of a society.

Put another way, secularisation is the process whereby religion loses its potency as an enterprise in world-building. Witness the rise of the modern secular state. Witness the plurality of alternative world-views available to us today. In fact, whereas religious traditions could impose their authority in times past, now religions have to be *marketed – sold* – to a clientele no longer under any constraint to *buy*. As Berger says, religious institutions have become marketing agencies and religious traditions have become consumer commodities.

A sacred canopy is a sacred canopy for the believer for as long as it is *plausible*. When the modernising processes we have been speaking about undercut the very grounding of one's belief in a 'sacred canopy', you have a crisis of *legitimation*. Secularisation means the gradual process by which sectors of society and culture are removed from the dominance, even domination, of religious institutions and symbols. And the 'carriers' (Berger) of this process have been the capitalist economy, industrialisation and the advent of science and technology.

Berger's 'crisis of credibility' in religion has led to what sociologists call the 'subjectivisation' or privatisation of religion. A student of the process of secularisation will say that in the marketplace of ideas you will find religions, ideologies and philosophies all vying for the attention of the modern soul in search of meaning. According to Berger, a virtual 'smorgasbord' awaits the modern enquirer – all claiming to offer answers to existential questions about the meaning of it all.

How would a philosopher who is a *naturalist* tackle a question like this? Remembering that a naturalist is someone who holds that we do not need a God, the gods, or the supernatural to understand how things hang together, broadly speaking. Enter Owen Flanagan.

I first encountered Flanagan, professor of philosophy at Duke University in the United States, now in his early 70s, when I came across a book of his when browsing at a book sale: *The Problem of the Soul* (2002). Written with non-philosophers in mind, it deals with the tough questions that follow the undermining of the 'sacred canopy' by secular modernity. What attracted me to his work at the time was the way he grounded his fascination with philosophy in his personal history. Irish and Catholic by upbringing, from the suburbs of New York City, he lost his faith as a young man when he could no longer accept Catholic teachings on morality.

He is a big-picture philosopher, at his prime, who has written a dozen books on consciousness, ethics and morality and the meaning of life. Flanagan argues that science raises compelling questions about consciousness and morality – really hard questions. A thorough-going naturalist, he argues that everything in the universe, including us, consists of physical matter governed by physical forces. But science doesn't and can't explain everything. Take morality or ethics. Yes, Darwinian natural selection has made us inherently selfish, but it has *also* made us loving, compassionate and empathetic, concerned with justice and fairness because these tendencies helped our ancestors pass on their genes.

And what about meaning? If you can no longer look to God and heaven for meaning and purpose in life, you still have much to live for, says Flanagan. At the time he wrote *The Problem of the Soul*, his personal life was in crisis; he was struggling with his own 'problem of the soul'. A brain tumour combined with medications that caused aberrant behaviour undermined his marriage and threw him into despair. Writing the book was part of his journey of recovery.

What caught my eye was the task Flanagan set himself. Science says that we are animals that evolved according to the principles of natural selection. It further claims that although we are extraordinary animals we possess no capacity that permits us to circumvent the laws of cause and effect.

What bothers Owen Flanagan is that no advocate of science has made an adequate effort to explain 'carefully, patiently and explicitly ... a robust conception of what it means to be a human person, a being possessed of consciousness, with the capacities for self-knowledge and the ability to live rationally, morally, and meaningfully'.

Tall order! Yes, indeed.

When it comes to understanding the modern self, there seems to be a broad scientific consensus about two things. First, we will need to 'demythologise' persons – we need to root out unfounded ideas. Take the idea of the soul, for instance, says Flanagan. We must let go of the belief in souls. There are no such things as souls, or non-physical minds. Although deeply entrenched, even in modernity, there is simply no warrant for the widespread belief in the soul or the mind which outlives death.

Second, we will need to 'think of persons as part of nature' – as natural creatures completely obedient and responsive to natural law. To put it bluntly, science has 'desouled' us, says Flanagan.

The cumulative discoveries of the human sciences in the last 150 years from psychology, sociology, anthropology, evolutionary biology, genetics, and neuroscience have fundamentally altered the way we understand ourselves. That's why we don't treat depression by extracting black bile anymore.

Cognitive science and neuroscience (Flanagan teaches philosophy and neuroscience) have reliable tools and methods for examining and understanding how the mind/brain works. We are, indeed, fully 'embodied creatures' according to Flanagan – the complex interplay of genes, culture and history makes us who we are.

But there is a certain modesty in these claims. It's not that we now fully understand human nature. Far from it. But we can say with confidence that we have a good sense of what needs to be explained.

And that goes for the hardest problem of all – human consciousness. According to Flanagan, no scientifically minded person thinks we will need resources beyond those available to genetics, biology, psychology, neuroscience, anthropology, sociology, history, economics, political science, and naturalistic philosophy to understand the nature of persons.

For philosophers like Owen Flanagan, who take the advent of science seriously and work within a naturalistic framework, human beings are not made in the image of God with intangible souls. Rather they are fully embodied creatures whose brain is the seat of selfhood. What is more, their sense of self develops by interacting with natural and social environments.

But, says Flanagan, most of us are uneasy about a merely scientific image of human beings. The uncomfortable feeling we have is because, if the science has its way, there would be no room for meaning and morals. With God out of the picture, we are deprived of theological answers to these questions. Where then do we look?

It's worth quoting Flanagan in full on this crucial question:

> We want our lives to have meaning and purpose, and we want the quest to do good and be good to make sense. But if we are just a very smart animal; if our earthly life is all we have; and if everything we believe, think, and value is in large measure the result of contingencies over which we have little control, then what, at the end of the day, is the quest to live a meaningful and good life even about?

49

What, indeed? One well-known Darwinist, Richard Dawkins, says we are simply replication machines for 'selfish genes'. Doesn't a naturalist have to concede that we are merely smart animals?

Here, Owen Flanagan makes a somewhat radical move. He draws on a tradition going back to Aristotle. We need to think of meaning and morals as forms of *ecology*. Aristotle didn't use the term 'ecology', but he insisted that human beings can flourish when they live in a healthy political system that promotes justice.

Ethics, broadly understood, includes meaning and morals. It is the systematic reflection on the conditions required for living the good life. And ecology is the science that studies how living systems relate to each other and their environment. By analogy, then, ethics can be seen as human ecology. What are the conditions under which human beings can flourish on this planet?

Of course, when you choose such a path you are in danger of scientism – the brash overreaching of the scientific doctrine which says that everything worth saying can be said in a scientific idiom. But we can, says Flanagan, avoid the pitfalls of scientism. It is patently crazy to say that the work of a Michelangelo, Da Vinci, Van Gogh, Cezanne or Picasso, of Mozart, Chopin, or Schonberg could be expressed scientifically.

If we take the analogy of ethical inquiry as ecology seriously, says Flanagan, then ethics can be conceived as empirical – an inquiry into the conditions that reliably lead to human flourishing. Put another way, it's not beyond our wit to enquire into those conditions which lead to human flourishing. Ethics as ecology aims, then, to describe, explain, and predict the behaviour which it studies. It is descriptive. But it is also a normative science. It implicitly trades in oughts. Beavers flourish in such and such environments; therefore, if you want to create a good habitat for beavers, you ought to do this and that.

What do we know about the conditions under which humans flourish? Ought we not to strive for those?

It took me a while to get my mind around the notion of ethics as ecology, of ethics as an *empirical* project. And for good reason. First, I was brought up to avoid what is called the 'naturalistic fallacy' – the idea that you can derive an 'ought' from an 'is'. You may be able to estimate with some degree of accuracy, scientifically that is, that there are five hundred thousand people living below the poverty-datum line in Cape Town. But it does not follow simply or easily from this fact that business corporations in Cape Town ought to do something about it. To make that argument you would have to make an *ethical* case for the corporate social responsibility of business.

Second, I was familiar with the notion of 'descriptive ethics' – describing, for instance, the moral customs and practices of people in rural India. But Flanagan appears to be saying something else.

Drawing on what he calls the rich tradition of secular ethicists in the West, beginning with Aristotle, Flanagan says that they seek to locate, describe, and discover the conditions of meaningful and good human lives. Aristotle had a word for this; 'flourishing', from the Greek word *eudaimonia*. Starting from this Aristotelian principle, what can we say about human flourishing? This is how Flanagan sees it:

> Meaningful lives ... involve being moral, having true friends, and having the opportunities to express our talents, to find meaningful work, to create and live among beautiful things, and to live cooperatively in social environments where we trust each other.

Thus, Flanagan claims we can conceive of meaning and morals without looking to divine law as set down by God in sacred texts. Ethics can be understood as an inquiry into the conditions under which people flourish. In short, 'we have minds, we are persons, and we have capacities to modify and control how we live.' We humans are creatures who want to live meaningfully and morally.

As the reviewer Tom Clarke noted, Owen Flanagan's *The Problem of the Soul* is revolutionary in its attempt to offer a reasoned and synoptic view of what a naturalistic view of human beings and human flourishing might look like. Flanagan has followed it up with a book called *The Really Hard Problem* in which he explores the problem of meaning, given the advances in neuroscience. And more recently with a book called *The Geography of Morals* in which he sets out to explore varieties of moral possibility.

Many years ago Jenny and I walked around the ancient city of York in the UK, guided by an audio cassette that gave us an idea of the sights and sounds of the city in medieval times. I remember thinking how glad I was that I didn't have to put up with the hardships of life then. We owe to science and technology the massive advances in public health, medicine, waste management and town planning that distinguish York the medieval city from the modern one.

Weber's 'disenchantment' is a sort of shorthand way of describing the process whereby magical thought and practice were eliminated by the development of science and technology. And I, for one, am glad to be a beneficiary of this process.

Disenchantment, in the sense I am using it, is the condition under which believer and secular naturalists live today. The modern world has been deeply and profoundly shaped by the idea of a natural order that can be understood without reference to anything outside itself. This is 'the great invention of the West'. It is the frame within which divine creation can be set aside.

Charles Taylor calls this taken-for-grantedness the 'immanent frame' which believers and non-believers share. This immanent frame profoundly changes our practical self-understanding, how we fit into our world and into society.

Given the comforts and consolations of religion, it is not difficult to understand the sense of loss, even lack, people feel when finally they are able to come to terms with the disenchantment of the world. Julian Barnes captures this when he writes, 'I don't believe in God but I miss Him.' Are we, then, staring into the abyss? Without meaning? Without purpose? Facing, finally, what Philip Larkin called 'extinction'?

... the total emptiness for ever,
The sure extinction that we travel to
And shall be lost in always. Not to be here,
Not to be anywhere,
And soon; nothing more terrible, nothing more true.

Yes, we must not confuse disenchantment with the end of religion – given the resurgence of religion world-wide, patently that would be false. But for those of us who find ourselves coming to terms with the 'immanent frame', living in a state of unknowing is precisely where we are. Out there, with questions which continue to haunt us and no easy answers.

But, using our sociological imaginations and our reason we can, as Owen Flanagan says, 'locate, describe, and discover the conditions of meaningful and good human lives.' Aristotle thought of *eudaimonia* as something you do: an activity, a *praxis*.

Interlude

My association with the Graduate School of Business had not been one-sided; I learned about the fraught area of mediation in industrial relations and cemented ties with new colleagues. But I also expressed concerns about the lack of *context* in MBA courses. Highly motivated and intelligent young people were being trained for management in South Africa blindfolded, with their hands tied behind their backs, because they had no understanding of the history of black politics and the trade union movement. The GSB responded by asking me to develop an elective course that could be presented as part of the MBA programme. It became a core MBA course, which I was to offer for the first time in 1980.

From teaching religion and society to undergraduates in Religious Studies, I found myself preparing to teach a 'business and society' course to MBA students. We studied the 'other' history of South Africa, which described the struggle against colonialism and apartheid – the one few MBA students would have learned about in white schools.

We read the Freedom Charter and discussed the fault line that ran through our country – the structural inequality and racism that apartheid masked but which any future, democratically elected government would have to grapple with. We looked at the challenges of doing business in an authoritarian society and debated the social responsibility of business. We learned to apply ethical theories to the South African case.

I taught jointly in Religious Studies and the GSB for a time, until I was appointed to the first chair in Social Ethics at a South African business school, in 1983. This unique experience forced me to come to grips with democratic theory, market economies and the powerful forces of modernisation that shape our world. Standing in front of MBA students, who, as future managers, were seeking to come to terms with the South African reality in an increasingly hostile world,

I experienced the full gambit of these forces. My first encounter with an MBA class was nerve-wracking: 75 students in tiered seats waiting … The GSB had made my course compulsory, but many students thought it was a soft option and were sceptical. I was outlining the course in my introductory remarks when a woman at the back of the class put up her hand. With a pronounced American accent – she was from Chicago – she said, 'All this is verbal masturbation; it has no place in a MBA!'

Later, I learned that she was a follower of Milton Friedman, the doyen of the Chicago school of economics, who believed that the sole purpose of a corporation was to make as much money for its shareholders as possible. Here was I, teaching that to do business in South Africa, you had to take seriously the political economy of apartheid – heresy to a Friedmanite.

What could be more secular than a business school? I had to rethink my approach. I couldn't assume that the students would share, or even understand, the Judaeo-Christian tradition that until then had informed my own thinking. In so far as I was conscious of the process going on inside myself, I was busy *translating* criteria for social choice, such as love, justice and truth from their explicitly Judaeo-Christian usage to the secular.

My guiding presuppositions were changing. Guiding presuppositions, as Niebuhr says, are like spectacles. To be able to see better I had to change my spectacles to suit my secular environment. Having the courage to do so opened up new vistas and introduced me to secular thinkers who grappled without the comforts and consolations of religion. For them, God was not a hypothesis to be resorted to when all else failed.

Fortunately, I discovered Charles Lindblom's book, *Politics and Markets: The World's Political-Economic Systems* (1977), and later met the man at Princeton University. Quietly spoken, with doctorates in economics and politics, and a passion for justice, he became my mentor in this new world of political economy. He enabled me to see the differences between despotic and democratic governments from the perspective of how they treat the market. The 'fundamental politico-economic alternatives open to man make up only a very short list', says Lindblom. 'One is social organisation through the authority of government.' Command economies such as the USSR or Cuba are examples. 'One is social organisation through exchange and markets.' Social democracies, like Sweden, and liberal democracies like the USA, come to mind.

Fascism, Nazism and apartheid are totalising systems of thought and practice. Charles Lindblom helped to me understand how these totalising systems work. They use knowledge to spin their webs of deceit and cause untold suffering. I have used Lindblom's 'Two Models' many times in my graduate classes. They became my bullshit monitor, alerting me to the dangers of closed systems.

Model One is an ideal type of a closed, authoritarian or totalitarian system. Here, an intellectually competent elite (the Party) is the custodian of a comprehensive theory of how things work and how change happens. The test of the theory is its correctness according to the canon of the political elite. The system is closed and a harmony of needs is assumed. It's a consensus model that tolerates no conflict; opposition is outlawed. The South African apartheid state was such a system. Elements of the ruling party, even today, exhibit Model One tendencies, I would argue. In management terms, a company practising top-down management that brooks little dissent exhibits attributes of a closed system.

Model Two is an ideal type of open system. Intellectual fallibility is assumed. No synoptic theory is therefore possible. There simply is no elite that knows how it all works. The test of policy is whether it is broadly willed and volition-driven, because the will of the people is the best guide to their wants and needs. Ends must be chosen from among alternatives. Competing needs and interests are inherent in the system. Any democratic country exhibits some or all of these characteristics. In management terms, a company that is attempting to be a learning organisation is of this type.

When I look back on this period, I realise that Lindblom's view of market economies is more benign than mine. It was important for MBA students, the future leaders of the capitalist system, to get to grips with the nature of the authoritarian apartheid system and its appetite for co-opting the market for its own oppressive ends. Contrary to what business believed, the apartheid system was a despotic planned economy. Business in South Africa was *not* operating in a free market system.

The world my MBA students were preparing themselves for was a 'disenchanted world' where strategies were developed, risks calculated, and plans made without reference to the supernatural. Commerce and industry, markets and technology innovation, risk assessment, balance of interests, mergers and acquisitions – all these vital aspects of a modern economy were thoroughly teleological. Ends were defined, and the most efficient means calculated to achieve them; implementation plans were made in the most *rational* way possible.

At the time, I was making sense of the secular world. I was compiling cognitive building blocks to enable me to grasp a world not premised on an agency view of God. Neither business nor science, neither politics nor economics required God to make them work. In the period since the Enlightenment, from around the late eighteenth century, science and its handmaiden, technology, have firmly established themselves as the pre-eminent tools of understanding the world. Add to them a political economy based on self-interest regulated by competition and you have a powerful brew – modernity. Nature and society (economy) operate by rules that can be discovered and exploited – a de-sacralised, secular world.

I quickly realised that a business school is a product of the Enlightenment, the period from the mid-seventeenth century through the eighteenth century that revolutionised science, philosophy, economics and politics in the West. That period when the Good, the True and the Beautiful were redefined. Where the *True* is what can be tested by experience, arrived at by the process of reason – modern science. Where the *Good*, what is morally right, is arrived at by reason not revelation, by utilitarian calculation of the greatest good, or by the rational imperatives of Immanuel Kant (1724-1804). Where the *Beautiful* in art, literature and music is assessed by means of the newly crafted tools of rational criticism.

A business school is also heir to what Robert Heilbroner called 'the worldly philosophers', the founding fathers of economics, of whom Adam Smith was the most famous. It's extraordinary, but until Adam Smith no philosopher had turned his or her mind to the mysteries of trade and commerce, to the political economy. He was a leading figure in the Scottish Enlightenment and taught moral philosophy at the University of Glasgow. In 1776, he published *An Inquiry into the Nature and Causes of the Wealth of Nations*. Now trade and commerce had an economic blueprint; the laws of the market had a philosophical underpinning. 'It is not from the benevolence of the butcher, the brewer, or the baker that we expect our dinner,' says Smith, 'but from their regard to their self-interest. We address ourselves, not to their humanity, but to their self-love, and never talk to them of our necessities, but of their advantage.' So, self-interest drives the market and competition regulates it.

My MBA students were mainly accountants and engineers. Few had any exposure to the humanities. It was important for them to understand the intellectual roots of modernity – my shorthand for the revolution brought on by the Enlightenment in the West.

A modernity that was secular in the sense that God was not an explanatory device. God was not to be found in the gaps between what we know and understand and what we don't know and don't understand about the world. God was not in the atom; he was not to be found in the tree or rock; he was not to be found in the sky;

he was not in any way to be identified with the world. I used two examples with my students: When a machine breaks down in the factory, there is no point in getting down on your knees and praying for it to be fixed; you call in a technician trained to fix it. When a child develops an inoperable cancer, there is no point in praying for God to beat the cancer. Paediatric oncology is the discipline that seeks to understand, along with the entire community of medical researchers, inoperable cancers in children.

While I was constantly engaged with these moral issues, there was not only a life of the mind to contend with. There was also the life of daily matters. I was finding it increasingly difficult to divide my time between teaching undergraduates in the Department of Religious Studies and postgraduates in the Graduate School of Business (GSB). My 50:50 joint appointment seemed to add up to two full-time appointments. So when the GSB created the chair in Social Ethics, I had to make a choice. The momentum of my short academic career was shifting. I reasoned that the introduction of applied ethics and business and society courses to the MBA curriculum was breaking new ground. And that it was important that business schools prepare young managers for the rigours of management in South Africa. So, I applied and was appointed to the first-ever chair in Social Ethics in a South African business school.

An inaugural lecture is an opportunity for a newly appointed professor to sketch his or her approach to his or her discipline. A daunting experience. A crowd of academics and members of the public, with a smattering of students, turned out for mine at UCT in 1984. My family was there. The formal occasion was presided over by the Vice Chancellor. The Dean and Head of Department were there, and John Cumpsty had been asked to give the vote of thanks.

Here was my chance to speak about the corporate social responsibility of business in South Africa's political economy, at a time when Milton Friedman's ultra-conservative views were becoming dominant in business. I argued that in apartheid South Africa corporate social responsibility was a subversive doctrine, but not for the reasons Friedman outlined. *Not* exercising social responsibility subverts business's best long-term interests and is morally indefensible. Why should society allow business to behave irresponsibly? Why should we accept an apolitical view of business as a non-player in the political economy? In a free market, corporations are major players. They exercise huge discretionary powers that shape society for good or ill. They can inject teargas or oxygen into the mine shaft of the economy. As such, they ought to be held accountable.

In democratic/free market societies, business and government are in a symbiotic relationship. The check on government, in theory, is at the ballot box. But where is the check on business? I argued that 'business ethics', or applied ethics in a business context, is one way in which business can exercise accountability. It's not good business, nor is it good for business, to indulge in unfair and discriminatory labour practices in a society as grossly unequal as South Africa under apartheid. Additionally, the degradation of the environment through toxic emissions from mines and factories could not continue unchallenged any more than business could remain silent in the face of unjust laws that spelled disaster.

The establishment of this chair was a sign that business was willing to take its corporate social and moral responsibilities seriously. Business schools in South Africa, I argued, ought to reflect on what constitutes 'an ethic of responsible action'.

The response to my inaugural lecture was mixed, as I expected. Some business leaders thought it too left-wing and not mainstream enough. Some applauded my approach, saying little had been done to give corporate social responsibility theoretical rigour. I was pleased that the university audience applauded it. John Cumpsty's vote of thanks was generous; he talked about the need for courage when speaking truth to corporate power.

The late 1970s and early 1980s were turbulent times in sub-Saharan Africa. This troubled environment heightened the ideological conflict in South Africa, and in the late 1970s led the South African Council of Churches (SACC) to commission a study of conflicting ideologies. A diverse group of people from different denominations, language groups and races was invited to serve on the commission. A core group met frequently and over a number of years before the commission's report was made public. I served on this commission and was editor-in-chief of the widely read book that published its findings in 1986, called *Contending Ideologies in South Africa.*

The idea was that the commission would report its findings in a way that would inform church leaders and concerned lay people. Initially the commission faced several challenges. Group members needed time to build trust. Then there was the challenge of how to approach ideology. No one in South Africa had attempted to enter these troubled waters.

After much debate, the commission concluded that it would not be possible to agree on a single normative theoretical, or even ideological, framework to identify and describe conflicting ideologies. Ideology is a slippery, contentious concept. And in South Africa people were dying for their ideological beliefs. So the commission opted for what we called a 'soft phenomenological' approach. It tried to describe ideologies in their own terms as a first step to grasping their irresistible appeal for some and the heated opposition they evoked in others. This implied that we had to bracket our own judgments on specific ideologies and deal with them descriptively – recognising that to describe something is already to intrude on what is being described. A strangely depoliticised position, no doubt, but we could see no other way.

We did introduce a critical perspective into our discussion by outlining, wherever possible, the way a particular ideology, such as Black Consciousness, was perceived from other ideological perspectives, such as liberalism or Afrikaner nationalism. In other words, we attempted to create the beginnings of a dialogue between ideologies in which they could begin to relativise each other.

The commission found it difficult to offer a theological critique of ideology – the third challenge. There was no single Roman Catholic or Protestant approach to ideology, let alone to capitalism, African socialism, or Afrikaner nationalism. Some argued that Christian theology itself was ideological in that it reflected thought and action in a particular setting. In the end, we presented two contrasting theological perspectives in our final chapter.

The challenges faced needed a long gestation – some five years in all. The stakes were high. On some estimates South Africa had entered its darkest hour. Repression and death at the hands of an increasingly authoritarian regime had become the order of the day. What was to be done? The churches participating in the SACC believed that one way to meet the challenges was to attempt to get people to come out of their entrenched positions through debate and dialogue. A futile endeavour, some would say, but one the commission tackled as best it could.

The first part of *Contending Ideologies in South Africa* dealt with the history and growth of capitalism, and with ideological critiques of South African capitalism. The second part dealt with liberalism, Afrikaner nationalism, African nationalism, Black Consciousness, and ethnic nationalism. Part three described socialism, Marxism and Communism in South Africa and Africa, and social democracy. Given the times and the prevailing ignorance about socialism, part four described the basic ideas of Marx, Marxism-Leninism, anarchism, Maoism in China, and trends in European Marxism. The final part of the book described our approach to ideology, and two approaches to the relationship between Christian theology and ideology.

The book proved surprisingly successful, becoming one of publisher David Philip's non-fiction bestsellers. It went into a second printing. I think it made an impact because it set out to *open* up debate on the ideological nature of our conflict at a time when South Africa was becoming an ever more *closed* society. Also, its methodology offered a way forward.

See if you can describe as fairly as possible what you understand by, let us say, Afrikaner nationalism, and then see if you can critique it from the perspective, say, of Black Consciousness. To achieve this, we needed a diversity of contributors. It was some feat to have Theo Kneifel, a radical Catholic, and Klaus Nurnberger, a liberal Lutheran, on the same commission as the centre-of-field John Cumpsty and Buti Thlagale, a Black Consciousness proponent, as well as Norman Bromberger, an atheist economist, and me – a liberal humanist.

My involvement in the commission on ideologies enabled me to bring current thinking and research to the GSB classroom discussions on the future of South Africa.

Only a few of us were working in the field of applied ethics in a business context in South Africa. Applied ethics is a branch of moral philosophy concerned with how we behave in specific contexts, and how we make decisions for ourselves, for others and for the future. Biomedical ethics, for example, is concerned with choices in such fields as genetic engineering, human fertilisation and behaviour control. Environmental ethics is concerned with ensuring a sustainable world for ourselves and our unborn neighbours. Political ethics is about justice and rights in political systems, development ethics with optimal strategies for sustainable growth and poverty reduction. For some years, I had been trying to craft a humanities approach to the branch of applied ethics called business ethics.

The notion of business ethics reduces some audiences to tears of laughter. Yet, it's a branch of applied ethics that has enjoyed a resurgence since the late 1980s. A glance at the literature reveals the wide range of topics in this growing discipline as it is taught until today in business schools in the USA, the UK and Europe. Course material contains case studies and discussions on issues of economic justice, corporate responsibility, government-business relations, conflict of interest/obligation in law, investment policy, advertising/marketing, environmental responsibility, human resource management and organisation.

How were we to tell this story during apartheid? What was the human resources (HR) director to do when the security police arrested the shop steward at his factory? Did he continue to pay the man, so his family didn't starve? If he did, the company was liable to incur the wrath of the establishment, even to lose government contracts. One way to deal with this, and the case is based on a real-life example from the Eastern Cape of the early 1980s, was to affirm the ethical principle that every employee must be considered innocent until proven guilty in a court of law. Since the shop steward had not been tried, the company didn't even know what he was alleged to have done, thus he ought to remain on the payroll.

This was not a simple case. Another ethical principle to consider was that the HR director ought to act so as to achieve the greatest good for the greatest number. Sacrificing one shop steward (and family) for the sake of the enterprise and all employed by it could be justified on utilitarian grounds.

I took the view that every day in the corporate board room, on the factory floor, in the trade union office and in the corridors of power, men and women of goodwill must make choices that affect the lives of people, the community and the enterprise.

The role of the humanities in classical Greece was to prepare young men for active citizenship in the 'polis', or city-state. In our world, business represents a strategic and substantive part of the state. Those who teach or approach business ethics from a humanities perspective seek to craft an approach that challenges decision-makers not to act with moral impunity, but out of a sense of care for the world.

Business ethics is multidisciplinary, drawing from such diverse disciplines as sociology, political economy, moral philosophy, history, jurisprudence, psychology, and decision theory. Its aim is

Weberian; it perceives leadership, in the public and private sectors, as a vocation in which the responsible exercise of power in and by organisations is an overriding moral imperative.

No practical man or woman (politician, bureaucrat, or manager) can avoid 'acting on the world', putting his or her 'hand to the wheel of history', as Weber said. Pursuing a policy of affirmative action, or re-engineering an organisation, or developing a reconstruction and development plan, is not a neutral act but a form of social engineering. It is the exercise of power, based, presumably, on policy, planning and strategic choice.

The test of a manager (or politician or bureaucrat) is not whether he or she has acted, but whether he or she does so with impunity. By impunity I mean a sense of exemption or immunity from unpleasant intended or unintended consequences. It means to act without care or heed of the consequences. This is true today and it was true during apartheid.

Bobby Godsell, to my mind, was an example of an ethical business leader. As industrial relations director for Anglo American, he took the decision to fire thousands of striking mineworkers when the union had rejected all avenues for a settlement. Cyril Ramaphosa was the General Secretary of the NUM at the time. Bobby told me that in matters of gravity 'you cannot act with impunity', 'I will carry responsibility for that fateful decision with me to my grave'. Yet the consequences of not acting could have crippled the mining house and the futures of many more thousands of workers and their families.

One of the difficulties with utilitarianism, which I would claim is the predominant ethic of most managers, is that it can be used to justify almost any action. As Machiavelli argued, the statesman (i.e., one who exercises power) may have to learn how *not* to be good – for example, by torturing a suspected terrorist, retrenching workers or indemnifying assassins. That does not justify torture, retrenchment or assassination. Not acting with impunity means taking responsibility for one's actions, living with dirty hands, facing the loss of innocence. One cannot exercise power innocently.

Max Weber, in his famous essay 'Politics as a Vocation' (1919), distinguished between two types of politically and socially relevant ethics – the 'ethics of ultimate ends', and the 'ethics of responsibility'. The pacifist or revolutionary, for example, insists on absolute values that cannot be compromised by outcomes. The ethics of responsibility is the anguished grappling of the actor seeking to effect the most humane consequences possible, even when the choices involve tragedy and pain.

Weber believed there is an 'elective affinity' between world-abnegation or denial and an absolute ethic, and between world-affirmation and an ethic of responsibility. In the one, the world can go to hell as long as the purity of ends is maintained. In the other, you are judged (by history) not by whether you acted, but by whether you acted out of a sense of care for the world, and are prepared to live with the consequences of your choices. Bobby Godsell was aware of this and acknowledged as much to Cyril Ramaphosa at the time.

Given his rich and insightful analysis, regrettably, Weber did not leave a developed 'ethic of responsibility' for those whose vocation it is to exercise power. That, no less, is our task as teachers and/ or practitioners, who reflect on what it means to exercise power with responsibility. In short, business ethics is about giving power a conscience.

Towards a moral GPS

All changed, changed utterly:
A terrible beauty is born.
– W. B. Yeats, 'Easter 1916'

All the while I was trying to develop co-ordinates for my moral GPS, co-ordinates to guide me while I was teaching ethics at the UCT and Wits business schools.

What is special about our time is that the ethical challenges are unique and unprecedented. We confront an ethical vacuum. Our use of science and technology has eroded our faith in the established moral traditions, religious and secular. Where do we find a moral compass, or GPS, to chart our way?

There has been a resurgence of religions; the majority of people in the world today are religious and do not experience the world as secular. However, religions crafted in the Iron Age seem inadequate for the challenges of the Information Age.

Advances in biotechnology enable humankind to alter human nature – to manipulate intelligence, biological sex, behaviour, even to prolong life. What do we do with the ability to annihilate the world through nuclear energy, global warming and the like? Part of what we mean by our time, or modernity, is that we are living through the dissolution of traditional values, with no agreement on how to construct new ones.

69

But let me step back for a minute. What is ethics? It helps me to think of ethics as a way of talking about our intentions and actions. Wittgenstein called the different ways of talking about facts, about beauty and about the good 'language games', likening them to the rules that apply to different board games. Just as the rules of chess and draughts are different, so too are the rules for talking about the empirical world of science, the aesthetic world of the arts, and the world of tough choices we call ethics. An example: during the Middle Ages, when plague was ravaging Europe, the prince of an Italian city ordered the walling-off of all houses where the dreaded disease had struck, including those whose occupants showed no signs of the disease. Everyone died in the walled-off part of the city, but the city itself was spared. Can I, who have spent much of my life taking down walls, judge whether the prince's action was morally justified? How would I do that?

Most people reluctantly come to view the prince's action as right in trying to save the city, even if it meant that innocents died. Many years later, Jeremy Bentham and John Stuart Mill formulated an approach to ethics called utilitarianism, based on the principle that we ought always to act in ways that reduce suffering. This principle, which I have touched on previously, is sometimes characterised by the phrase 'the greatest good or happiness of the greatest number'.

Others, however, are uncomfortable with licensing the prince to sacrifice the citizens of his city state for the greater good. The end doesn't justify the means, in this case, or indeed in any other. The prince's action cannot therefore be morally justified. The commandment 'Thou shalt not kill', found in Judaism, Islam, and Christianity, has universal appeal even when people no longer adhere to the faith. Moral imperatives such as 'killing is wrong' or 'lying is wrong' have the feel of commandments.

Immanuel Kant called this feature of ethical language a 'categorical imperative'. Kant's categorical imperatives share three characteristics. First, an act must be 'universalisable' to be moral. 'Thou shalt lie' fails this test. Truth telling is universalisable; telling lies is not. Second, always treat people as ends and never as a means to some end. Third, for an act to be moral it must be possible to do it.

If you observe the language game of ethics when it is idling, you can see that ethical language is not the same as, say, scientific language, or the language of aesthetics. In science, facts are everything. You measure and observe, and you test hypotheses until you are fairly certain that what you say about the observable world is true. True even for the twentieth century's greatest intellectual adventure, the advances in theoretical physics that gave us quantum theory and the special and general theories of relativity – though often the experimental verification of theories in physics cannot be tested for years because the technology doesn't exist.

Facts get you only some of the way in the discourse of ethics. We know that global warming threatens our fragile planet. But it does not follow that you and I ought to do something to save Planet Earth. Today we have better-quality scientific evidence that if we continue with present consumption patterns, we put the planet gravely at risk. But to make a convincing ethical argument for responsible stewardship of our natural world we need to begin elsewhere. We need a discussion about our duty towards nature. We need to devise an ethical argument for caring for our planet.

A key word in the language game of ethics is the word 'ought' in its various forms. Ought implies duty or obligation. Look up the word in the *Concise Oxford Dictionary* and you will find it means 'duty'. Look up 'duty' and you will find it means moral or legal 'obligation'. Look up 'obligation'; it means duty – something you *ought* to do because the law says so or because it is a moral or ethical imperative. You could say that the language game of ethics is circular; it doesn't matter where I start; at some point I will confront the word 'ought' and will need to invest it with particular meaning.

You might say that for the Jew, the Muslim, or the Christian the word ought is invested with meaning derived from the tenets of his or her faith. Yet even then, matters are not straightforward. The Torah, the Koran and the Bible are silent about biotechnology, euthanasia, stem cell research and global warming. There are well-meaning Jews, Muslims, and Christians on both sides of the contemporary debate about pressing ethical challenges such as abortion, capital punishment and birth control, drawing their inspiration from their sacred texts. The situation is further complicated. While most ancient traditions enshrine their basic values in their sacred texts, traditional ethical teachings are essentially ethics of proximity, about good neighbourliness. Examine the ethical precepts of Judaism, Islam, Christianity, Hinduism or Buddhism and you will find much wisdom about how to treat members of one's immediate family, one's neighbourhood and one's village.

There is a rabbinical story in which a man says he will become a believer if the Rabbi can recite the whole Torah while standing on one leg. The Rabbi stands on one leg and replies, 'That which is hateful to you, do not unto another: This is the whole Torah. The rest is commentary.'

You will also find much wisdom, hammered out over centuries of conflict, on how to deal with outsiders. Hans Jonas says of these traditions that the 'ethical universe is composed of contemporaries', the future 'is confined by the foreseeable span of their lives' and the horizon of place 'within which the agent and the other meet [is] as neighbour, friend or foe, as superior or subordinate, weaker or stronger'.

The reach of modern ethical issues confronting our global village, however, far outstrips the grasp of these venerable traditions.

The advent of modern technology and weakening of the efficacy of traditional ethical systems combine to map out the terrain on which we must act today to survive, even perhaps to flourish.

The key question for modernity, then, is this: where does the authority of the ought lie? If God is dead, is not anything permissible? What characterises modernity is moral dissensus. How do you decide right and wrong without a sacred text to guide you (Torah, Koran, Bible) or a moral authority to tell you what to do (Jesus, Buddha, or Marx)? Which right are we talking about anyway? Whose justice? Which rationality do we follow here – utilitarianism or Kant?

It seems that we are without a moral compass, a moral GPS.

I am aware this is not the whole picture. There is a considerable body of national and international convention and law, elaborated over the years and often at great cost. These define rights and obligations in areas such as labour and human rights. There are international conventions covering fairness in war, care of the environment, and the like. I think of the ILO, the WHO, UNICEF, NATO. These international conventions express our collective sense of what is right. Our moral ecology.

A democracy is an amalgam of lively, independent and competing institutions that reflect social compacts and conflicts of interest. It seeks tolerable balances of power or social equilibriums. An industrial relations system is one such institution, a strong civil society another. And these balances are expressed in our conventions and, ultimately, in our laws.

So, all is not moral dissensus.

But, if my experience in classrooms around South Africa is anything to go by, we do lack a common sense of 'the good', or even of how to construct it.

We need wisdom most when we have lost faith in its traditional sources. Our choices affect the lives of our unborn neighbours. We need what Hans Jonas calls 'a new ethics of long-range responsibility, coextensive with the range of our [technological] power'. One, he adds, that is characterised by humility.

One focus of my intellectual odyssey has been how to grapple with ethical issues outside the confines of the faith traditions – in the secular world. Over the years that I taught ethics, I researched the ethics helplines that thoughtful moderns have constructed to assist us to meet the challenges of our time.

Hans Jonas offers a great start. A classics scholar who escaped from Nazi Germany, Jonas (1903–1993) fought on the side of the Allies in the Second World War. His mother died in Auschwitz. He retooled himself and devoted his life to the challenges of technology, to the survival of the planet. In the search for the Good after Auschwitz and the Holocaust, Jonas began to develop an argument for the moral imperative of long-range responsibility towards our planet. Let me briefly share a sense of his nuanced argument in his book *Mortality and Morality: A Search for the Good after Auschwitz* (1996).

First, we ought – there's that word again – to accept long-range responsibility for our world. While we lack a crystal ball to look into the future, if we continue to behave as we do now, we put the planet at risk. We need to hone our predictive skills by all means possible. Second, we need to develop 'the heuristic of fear', to train ourselves to clearly see the consequences of actions now for the future of our world. 'We know the thing at stake only when we know that it is at stake', says Jonas. We know much sooner what we do *not* want than what we want. So, says Jonas, we must consult our fears prior to our wishes. We have no right to wager the interests of others, including our unborn neighbours, without their consent.

Third, we ought to accept responsibility for tomorrow because nature, including human nature, is intrinsically valuable. In short, we are stewards of the future of the world. 'Care for the future of mankind is the overruling duty of collective human action' in this technological age, says Jonas. The peril of war – nuclear, conventional or terrorist – is often cited as the peril of our time. Whether or not we will face such a peril is a function of arbitrary choice. Much more insidious is the slow, incremental threat posed by over-population and over-consumption 'whose ticking so far cannot be checked'.

Jonas is cautiously upbeat about our ability to 'govern technology'. Others, such as John Gray, are more pessimistic. In *Straw Dogs* (2002), Gray argues that 'humanity will never master technology' because 'humanity doesn't exist … only humans, driven by conflicting needs and illusions, and subject to every kind of infirmity of will and judgement', organised into nearly two hundred sovereign states, thereby making 'technology ungovernable'. More disconcerting still, he says, 'If anything about the present century is certain, it is that the power conferred on "humanity" by new technologies will be used to commit atrocious crimes against it.' Thought-provoking stuff.

How do we endeavour to live authentically in the modern world? Charles Taylor has spent much of his intellectual energy trying to understand the making of modern identity and what it might mean to live authentically.

Taylor carefully traces the sources of the 'self' in Western thought: how we have come to be individuals in our own right; how we have come to live in a disenchanted world no longer subject to the whims of gods or demons. This is the world of instrumental reason, where we calculate the most efficient means to achieve our ends.

Taylor argues that inherent in the making of modern identity is a complex tapestry of ideas and values that constitute the good life. We are not without a moral compass. On the contrary, we can construct an 'ethics of authenticity' by retrieving from the past the best insights that have shaped modernity. Indeed, there are clusters of ideas and intuitions that have the quality of commands or moral imperatives to the modern ear. Here are some of the fruits of Taylor's own exercise of retrieval.

First, says Taylor, there is the cluster of moral imperatives that include 'respect for life, integrity, and wellbeing, even the flourishing of others'. Then there is the obligation of benevolence that we feel as moderns – the imperative to reduce human suffering, including the suffering of all sentient beings. This is what informed the utilitarianism of Bentham and Mill.

Taylor describes another cluster of imperatives as the 'affirmation of ordinary life'. This includes production; the making of things needed for life, as well as reproduction – our life as sexual beings, including marriage and the family. Not only does ordinary life have value, so too does nature. Indeed, the affirmation of nature as an end in itself, as having intrinsic value, is a key moral imperative of our time. Then there is the cluster of values that emerge from the collapse of social hierarchies. These include equality, moving away from ascribing status to persons based on race, colour, class, gender or creed. Respect for human dignity and the freedom of the individual as universal are another cluster. It is these values of equal recognition that usher in democracy.

This rings true for me. I think what Taylor is saying is that, if I key into my moral GPS the co-ordinates that have been refined over the years, I will find direction. My way home. I ought to respect life, seek the wellbeing of others, even their flourishing. I ought to affirm the value of this life, and of nature itself. I ought to treat others as ends in themselves, not as means – not, that is, according to their race, class, gender or creed. It's an exercise in retrieval, certainly, but it can guide me when I am perplexed, wondering how I should act. Commandments that come down from a different mountain.

Given the levels of poverty and inequality in modern times, what are our chances of creating just or fair societies? John Rawls of Harvard University is possibly the most frequently cited English-language philosopher of the twentieth century. His book *A Theory of Justice*, published in 1971, caused a storm that has yet to abate. Certainly, we debated his book robustly in MBA classes. Let me offer you a flavour of Rawls's project. He sets out to answer the question, 'What sort of arrangement would we choose, if we were positioned to make a choice, to create a just and fair society to live in?'

Consider this 'thought experiment'. You are behind a 'veil of ignorance' concerning your place in society. You don't know, behind this veil of ignorance, whether you are black or white, rich or poor, male or female, intelligent or not. You do, however, understand politics and the principles of justice. You understand the basic principles of economics. You have a sense of how social organisation works and the basic principles of human psychology. In other words, you don't know your place in society but you are a reasonably informed citizen. Now, says Rawls, behind the veil of ignorance, how would we decide on the socio-political arrangements we ought to have? In particular, how would we know which arrangement can claim to be just or fair, properly balancing our competing claims and interests?

Rawls sets out to establish what moral principles should govern. His answer is that without knowing our place in society, in our thought experiment, behind the veil of ignorance, we would finally choose to be governed by two principles.

First, there is the principle of equal rights to the most wide-ranging system of basic liberties for all (i.e. freedom of thought, speech, association and worship, etc.).

Since personal, social and economic goods are unequally distributed in all known societies, past and present, Rawls's second principle is controversial. Social and economic inequalities are to be arranged so that they are both:

a) to the greatest benefit of the least advantaged; and

b) attached to offices and positions open to all under conditions of fair equality of opportunity.

A great deal of ink has been spilled in the scholarly and popular press debating John Rawls's theory of justice as fairness. Now you can join the debate. How would you decide, if you could, and if you didn't know whether you were at the top of the pile or the bottom, the principles of a fair society?

What Rawls demonstrates is that we are not without a moral compass. We can apply our minds to such questions as justice and fairness. His intuition is that, if we were pressed, we would want to say a fair society is one in which the least advantaged are not forever condemned to remain just that, the least advantaged. Makes you think, doesn't it?

In the middle part of the twentieth century writers like Albert Camus and Simone de Beauvoir rebelled against moral rule-making, arguing that life is too complex and messy for rules. Both names are associated with existentialism, a loose term for various philosophers and thinkers who were reacting to the disillusionment in Europe in the aftermath of the Second World War. They emphasised individual responsibility, the need to make tough choices and our apparent inability to make rational sense of a world in which the Holocaust and Hiroshima are realities. Acting authentically, having made one's best judgment of what to do, are common themes with these authors.

Albert Camus (1913–1960) was born and raised in Algeria in a poor family, worked in the Paris underground movement during the Second World War and won the Nobel Prize for literature. His novels, plays and essays grappled with contemporary issues as well as the philosophical problem of meaning. A thoroughly modern man. He is described as the conscience of his time, specifically for his stance during the German occupation and in relation to France's colonial war in Algeria. Tragically, he was killed in a road accident in 1960. He is one of my intellectual heroes.

His early book, *The Myth of Sisyphus* (1942), written in France during the Second World War, opens thus: 'There is only one truly serious philosophical problem and that is suicide. Judging whether life is or is not worth living amounts to answering the fundamental question of philosophy.' Camus concludes that life is 'absurd', but that it is worth living for all that. Absurd because our demands for rationality and justice confront an 'indifferent universe' that is deaf to our pleas.

In the Greek myth, the gods condemned Sisyphus to roll a rock to the top of a mountain, only to watch it fall back under its own weight and his impotence. The gods thought nothing could be more dreadful a punishment than to be condemned to this futile, hopeless – yes, absurd – labour. Yet Sisyphus thrives, he is even happy, because of his scorn and defiance of the gods. His rebellion is what gives meaning to his life. In an age of anxiety, despair and nihilism,

Camus claims it is possible to have confidence in the future. If we decide to live, it must be because we have chosen that life is worth living. But the value we give to life, the personal choice we make, is not a given – not a trick played on us by religion or philosophy.

And, in a later essay, called *The Rebel* (1951), Camus argues that if we rebel (against the totalising ideologies of our time), it must be because we have opted for life in human society as worthwhile. This, too, is not a given. It's a choice we make.

So, for Camus, we may not win the first prize but we can strive for the second. This has been described as Camus's ethics of the second prize. As he famously said: 'Perhaps we cannot prevent the world from being a world in which children are tortured. But we can reduce the number of tortured children.'

We are seldom, if ever, confronted by choices between the absolutely right or absolutely wrong. Most times we operate in a grey area of ambiguity, paradox and uncertainty, and have to live with the consequences of our choices and actions.

Simone de Beauvoir's (1908-1986) *The Ethics of Ambiguity* (1947) explores these same themes. In the aftermath of the Second World War and the destruction wreaked by totalitarian systems such as Nazism and Communism, existentialist thinkers turned their minds to a radical understanding of freedom. There can be no fixed qualities, values, or tenets. The future is open; it is what we make of it. In the absence of fixed values and beliefs, we are called upon to embrace ambiguity and uncertainty.

All this is nicely illustrated in De Beauvoir's most famous book, *The Second Sex* (1949). Passive acceptance of the role into which women have been socialised is what De Beauvoir calls 'immanence' and it perpetuates gender inequality. Actively and freely testing one's possibilities with a view to redefining one's future is what she terms 'transcendence'. Historically, women have been consigned to immanence. But, says De Beauvoir, a woman is something one 'becomes' that transcends immanence. For existentialist thinkers like Camus and De Beauvoir, adherence to any totalising system is dangerous because you cede your freedom to the system and its controllers. Freedom, too, is dangerous, uncertain and ambiguous – even absurd. Our choice is whether we act out of care for the world, even if we feel like Sisyphus in doing so.

Practical wisdom is shorthand for the human capacity to take the right courses of action intuitively, mindfully, and responsibly.

When it comes to practical wisdom it is worth looking east, to the wisdom traditions such as Taoism and Buddhism that I discovered late in my life. What has surprised me is the convergence between the wisdom of the East, attained through millennia of contemplative practice and insight into human consciousness, and recent advances in neuroscience and cognitive science in the West.

Here I want to draw on the work of a leading representative of neuroscience and cognitive science, Francisco Varela, and the work of Stephen Batchelor, a former monk in the Tibetan and Zen traditions. In *Verses from the Center: A Buddhist Vision of the Sublime* (2001), Batchelor argues that at the heart of Buddhism is the counterintuitive recognition of human experience as 'radically transient, unreliable, and contingent'. The Buddha's great insight was that there is no essential self, no ghost in the machine, which orchestrates the array of experiences we have in each moment of consciousness. Life is just 'a dazzlingly tentative array of contingent processes, playing themselves out in complex sequences of causes and effects but with no discernible beginning and no divine power mysteriously directing them to a pre-ordained end.' The Buddha, says Batchelor, found this 'revelation of a selfless and Godless reality to be deeply liberating'.

In 1992, Francisco Varela published a slim book called *Ethical Know-How: Action, Wisdom and Cognition*. Here he ventures into the field of ethics, drawing on the latest neurobiology and cognitive science and what he calls the 'wisdom tradition' of the East. Ethics, says

Varela, is 'closer to wisdom than to reason, closer to understanding what is good than to correctly adjudicating particular situations.' He is interested in 'ethical know-how' rather than 'ethical know-what'.

According to Varela, modern neuroscience and cognitive science agree that what we call the self is really a 'micro identity' engaged with a 'micro world'. Our micro-worlds and micro-identities 'do not come all stuck together in one solid, centralised unitary self, but arise and subside in a succession of shifting patterns.' And, says Varela, we *develop* the know-how to act ethically – we acquire moral skill or expertise.

This position is not that different from what the Eastern wisdom traditions have been teaching for thousands of years, claims Varela. Human nature is capable of flourishing and growing; it is not stained by the Fall and original sin. Each of us is capable of becoming good, with training and cultivation of the mind.

Ethics, then, becomes a practical skill, and is understood as the knack of knowing what to do when confronted by the need to act. More like practical wisdom than learning the rules, as in duty-based ethics, or doing a cost-benefit analysis, as in utilitarianism.

The wisdom traditions of the East all place emphasis on developing the art of meditation, on training the mind. 'We are what we think,' says Buddha. 'All that we are arises with our thoughts; with our thoughts we make the world.' Now, Buddhists are not saying that if you meditate you will know intuitively how to act when confronted by moral choice. What they are saying is that if you meditate mindfully you will learn empathy, compassion and love for all sentient beings. You will learn to place yourself selflessly at the service of others. Says Batchelor, you will hear the wordless cry of the Other that forms the foundation of Buddhist ethics: do not kill me, do not rob me, do not abuse me, do not deceive me, do not betray me, do not insult me, do not waste my time, do not try to possess me, do not bear me ill will, do not misconstrue me.

In short, you will act out of a sense of care for the world.

Of course, Batchelor and Varela are talking about modern Buddhism. What about traditional Buddhism? It came as something of a surprise to me to discover that there is no word in Buddhist languages, such as Sanskrit, Pali and Tibetan, that exactly corresponds to the English word 'ethics'. The closest seems to mean something more like 'moral discipline'. Traditionally, Buddhist 'ethics' is about *intention*. As one authority put it, 'There are many contexts in which Buddhism seems to emphasise the intention with which an act was performed much more than the benefit or harm that actually resulted.' A case often cited is that of Channa, who presented a gift of food to the Buddha which gave him dysentery and thus caused his death. Since Channa's intention was to perform an act of generosity, the (dying) Buddha tells his followers not to condemn Channa.

According to Peter Harvey, a key general criterion of whether an action is wholesome/skilful (Pali *kusala*, Sanskrit *kusala*) is to look at its 'root' (*mula*) or impelling cause/motive: 'an act is unwholesome if rooted in greed, hatred or delusion, and wholesome if rooted in non-greed (generosity or renunciation), non-hatred (lovingkindness or compassion), or non-delusion (wisdom).'

Motivation rather than consequences. It is for this reason that some scholars speak of Buddhist 'ethics' as virtue ethics. In Western philosophy, virtue ethics is about the actions that flow from the kinds of people we are and strive to be, from the virtues we seek to cultivate in ourselves.

Buddhist ethics is the subject of continuing debate among scholars. One thing is certain, ethics as we know it in the West is enriched by this debate, and, I have no doubt, Buddhist ethics also benefits from its contact with Western moral philosophy.

Adi Ophir is an Israeli professor of philosophy at Tel Aviv University. Two major events in modern Jewish history have influenced his thinking: the Holocaust and the prolonged domination of Palestinians in the Occupied Territories. Ophir's book, *The Order of*

Evils, published in 2005, took nearly a decade to write. On the cover, Moshe Halbertal described it as 'the most sustained and brilliant philosophical discussion of evil' he had ever read.

This major contribution to a thoroughly secular understanding of Evil, has made a huge impact on me. You will not find the word 'devil' or 'Satan' in the extensive index. Ophir argues that evil is neither something diabolical in the hearts of men and women nor is it the meaningless absence of the good. Rather, it is *socially constructed*. The 'evil things that make people's lives bad: pain, suffering, loss, humiliation, damage, terror, alienation' arise, says Ophir, because 'people cause other people many evils – intentionally and unintentionally, knowingly and unknowingly, alone and in company with others'.

Ophir 'aims to position Evil in human history, in historical forms of social existence, and to attribute to human beings full responsibility for what they do to other human beings, without letting them escape to heaven or hell'. And that is his real contribution. The book is long: nearly seven hundred pages of carefully constructed argument. His aim is to change the paradigm by which we view the evils visited upon human beings, or the aggregate of evils that we call Evil.

And here is how he does it. A large proportion of these evils are what he calls 'superfluous', in the sense that they are 'preventable, and if they are not preventable then at least the suffering and damage they cause can be reduced. Superfluous evils that can be prevented or reduced should be reduced', he argues. 'Evil is the order of superfluous evils in society.' When someone is indifferent to superfluous evils, 'he expresses an immoral attitude'.

Ophir sets out to refocus the way we think about ethics. He presents a moral theory that is a mundane, secular answer to an old, mainly theological, question: what is Evil and what is its source?

His secular response, he says, displaces the centre of the debate from theology (How could Evil exist in a world created by an omnipotent, benevolent God?) and psychology (Is man born evil? Precisely where does Evil reside in man?) to sociology, political economy, political science, geography and ecology. This displacement is another step in the secularisation process of Western thought that began with modernity.

I remember reading many years ago a sermon by Helmut Thielicke. It was about the Old Testament story of the Fall, about our age-old disposition to pass the buck. When Adam is confronted by God, he says, don't blame me, it was Eve, the woman you gave me. She convinced me to pluck the forbidden fruit. Eve says, it's not my fault, it was the serpent who beguiled me. The serpent, in turn, says, I can't be held responsible. After all, God, did you not make me what I am?

When the problem of evil is framed in theological terms, it is easy to pass the buck. While engaging in the blame game, we absolve ourselves from responsibility. Adi Ophir will have none of this. Auschwitz was not a historical accident, Hiroshima was not a necessity of war, the Gulag was not an unintended consequence. These exemplars of superfluous Evil in the twentieth century were preventable – the suffering and damage they caused were avoidable. There is no agency (or Agency), no one to whom the buck can be passed. The buck stops with us.

In lighter vein, from *Plato and a Platypus Walk into a Bar* (2007) by Thomas Cathcart and Daniel Klein:

DIMITRI:	*I've been thinking about your question, what does 'good' mean, and I've got the answer – 'good' is acting on a just principle.*
TASSO:	*By Zeus, Dimitri, you're full of surprises – you're starting to sound like a real philosopher. Just one last question: How do you determine just principles?*

DIMITRI: *Du-uh! Just like everyone else. I learn them from my mom.*

TASSO *(aside):* *Why does Socrates get all the 'A' students?*

Interlude

I was enjoying the cut and thrust of teaching at the business school and the creative work of crafting an approach to business ethics in our fraught society. In some ways, I regret taking the next call.

It came from Stuart Saunders, the Vice Chancellor of UCT during those dark days of the 1980s when state repression in South Africa was at its height. I had first met Saunders when he was Acting Vice Principal, Planning and I was on the executive of the Lecturers' Association (LA). The LA was a powerful lobby. We proposed the introduction of a merit award for senior lecturers who were good scholars but were unlikely to be promoted and who bore the brunt of undergraduate teaching. After first expressing some scepticism, Saunders supported the proposal.

Now Saunders was Principal and Vice Chancellor. UCT was a centre of liberal activism and was often in crisis as the university community protested vigorously against the further inroads into human rights and freedoms that were the hallmark of the times. The university found itself in the teeth of the storm. Saunders asked me to become a locum, standing in for each of his deputy vice chancellors in turn to allow them to take a well-earned break, a scheme that also gave him time off.

Why did I take the job? First, I believed that UCT, an important liberal university, was endangered. There were incessant attacks on its integrity as a university. Second, it is one thing to teach social ethics and another to practise it. Being a locum meant that I spent time in a line management position, giving direction to key areas of university management, such as academic affairs, human relations and student affairs. At the end of my six-month locum period, the University Council was persuaded that an additional deputy vice chancellor (DVC) was needed. I was formally appointed to this position and spent nearly six years as part of the senior management of the university, from mid-1985 until early 1991.

These were dark and difficult times. And education was a flashpoint. Roughly a decade after the Soweto Uprising of 1976, two draconian states of emergency were declared as the country moved ever closer to becoming a national security state. It was a time of unremitting protest and unrest and increasingly oppressive pushback from the apartheid state.

I found myself doing what in business school jargon is called crisis management. The first crisis happened as I took office: the 1985 declaration of a state of emergency. It was midyear and most of the executive team was off campus. I was holding the fort. The university community was galvanised into action. A huge protest meeting was held in the Jameson Hall where I spoke on behalf of the VC.

'How shall we respond to this crisis in our nation?' I asked. 'We must go back to our roots and reaffirm the tradition and values which make this university great.' We must also 'address certain imperatives to the state', and 'renew our commitment as a university community.'

I pleaded that government use force responsibly and called for a quick end to the emergency. As a country 'we cannot fight our way out of the crisis we face,' I argued. I called for 'the politics of negotiation.' I urged that government 'heed the call of responsible leaders in public life and the private sector for the release of Nelson Mandela and other political detainees, the lifting of the ban on political organisations such as the ANC, and an amnesty to enable political exiles to return. The politics of negotiation can succeed only if it is conducted with the true representatives of the people.'

When I returned home, Jenny could see I was stressed but exhilarated. I felt I had led from the front. UCT had made a strong and impassioned plea for the country to move from the politics of violent confrontation to the politics of negotiation.

But the crisis deepened. My portfolios included student affairs, industrial relations and academic staffing. The human side of the enterprise. On any given day, students or staff or the trade union could be marching in protest. Often they combined. Often the marches turned ugly when riot police threatened the peaceful protests. Sometimes student protests ended violently and people were hurt and students incarcerated.

I was teargassed more times than I can remember. Most days, I had a two-way radio at my side. On one occasion, riot police stormed the upper campus to disperse protesting students, despite my efforts to prevent this. All hell broke loose. And, as I had predicted to the head of the riot squad, the students dispersed as teargas canisters exploded everywhere. They knew the campus better than the police did. The students regrouped and showered the police with rocks. Already struggling to see through the teargas, I nearly got stoned. How no one was seriously injured that day I'll never know.

Then there was that truly scary occasion when Stuart Saunders and I were with the mass of students protesting below the sports centre on the banks of De Waal Drive. A large contingent of heavily armed riot police gathered across the two-way highway. I could sense the tension on both sides. One student lobbing even a toilet roll could spark a violent response from the police. Stuart turned to me and asked what I thought we should do. 'We should both cross to the middle of De Waal Drive and stand on the island, between the students and the police,' I said. And so we did. Nerve-wracking – until the head of the riot squad invited us to join him and we were able to negotiate the withdrawal of the police on condition that the students withdrew.

During my tenure, UCT took the bold step of recognising industrial relations as one of the few ways in which black staff could express their political aspirations. UCT signed a historic Recognition Agreement with the University and Allied Workers' Union which included the right to strike. And we came perilously close to strike action. At the eleventh hour, once we and the Union had grasped what withholding labour could mean in a university, we were able to settle. But not before Union General Secretary Ebrahim Patel and I had taken a walk in the Newlands Forest to try to find a way forward. At the time of writing, Patel is Minister of Trade and Industry in the Cabinet of the ANC Government. The academic boycott had been in place since the 1970s. It received fresh impetus in the 1980s when it was supported by a special resolution of the United Nations. At UCT, it translated into the fact that the life-giving exchange of ideas and people between us and the rest of the world was constrained. Already hard-pressed, open universities like UCT were having to do more with less. Our library system was especially hard-hit.

Academic freedom is a cherished value at UCT. And in the midst of everything, it was seriously threatened by what came to be known as the 'Connor Cruise O'Brien Affair'. In October 1986, O'Brien, an Irish politician and academic, was invited to lecture at UCT. Some of his lectures were disrupted by students protesting against his visit because he had ignored the academic boycott, calling it a 'Mickey Mouse affair'. I was part of Saunders's team which faced an angry student protest at an evening public O'Brien lecture which we had to call off because we could not guarantee the safety of life, limb or property. Things quickly escalated. The VC informed him that his safety could not be guaranteed and O'Brien agreed to cancel his lectures at UCT. The event split the university. Many argued that UCT was honour-bound to uphold freedom of speech and conscience. Others argued that O'Brien was perceived to be dismissive of the fact that black South Africans, students included, were denied their basic human rights. It took the Senate an entire day to formulate a response to the crisis. Later it turned out that much of the student response to O'Brien was influenced by a policeman masquerading as a student and by student spies, acting as agents provocateurs to foment unrest on campus.

UCT faced its gravest threat yet from the State whilst I was DVC. At the time, South African universities enjoyed relative autonomy, were partially state-funded, and were governed by statute and by Councils. In August 1987, F. W. de Klerk informed all universities that legislation was being drafted to impose conditions on the award of state subsidies. If universities failed to curb protests, they would be penalised financially. Essentially, this was a move to co-opt universities to maintain 'law and order' on their campuses. The open universities mounted strenuous protests. International outrage followed. UCT and the University of the Western Cape (UWC) instituted a legal challenge to the De Klerk Conditions. Three judges of the Cape Supreme Court found in our favour and denied the Minister's application to appeal. A narrow escape.

For a liberal, open university like UCT there were many questions. How to ensure that the doors of learning were kept open? That the university decided on academic grounds alone who was to teach, as well as who and what was to be taught? Apartheid legislation blocked black student access to UCT. Black students were supposed to go to state-run black universities. After he took up his post as VC in the early 1980s, Stuart Saunders took the fateful decision to open university residences to black students, in breach of the Group Areas Act. Thus enabling student access to UCT for all South Africans.

Opening access like this meant that the university had to develop creative ways to fund students and to assist them to realise their full academic potential. Black students admitted over the years of my stay at UCT were able to access student financial aid and participate in academic support programmes to help them overcome the deficits of poverty and poor schooling. On-campus student housing had to be found, and quickly. In those early years, UCT began a process of social transformation that is ongoing.

I remember well the graduation dinner for engineering students and their parents which included black graduates – a first for UCT and, I think, for South Africa. I was sitting next to a very proud father from rural Eastern Cape. He had obviously been coached by his son on the etiquette involved in a formal dinner, the label of his new suit still attached to his sleeve. His son was a product of the opening of student access to UCT; he was supported by a special student financial aid scheme, schooled in a newly crafted academic development programme specially designed for entrants to engineering studies, and lived in a UCT hall of residence despite the laws forbidding this. From a rural upbringing to an engineering graduate all in one generation.

The executive management team was made up of an impressive group of top academics and managers committed to safeguarding one of South Africa's premier universities in those climactic times. It was a great privilege to be part of that team. And it prepared me for what lay ahead.

UCT was one of a small number of South African liberal universities that included Natal, Wits and Rhodes. In the late 1990s, the University of Natal (UN) was looking for a vice chancellor. Unbeknown to me I was nominated. After some soul-searching, Jenny and I allowed my nomination to stand. It was with some trepidation that I did so; I'd had first-hand experience of the demands of the job.

Why did I do this? I don't consider myself an ambitious man but I admit to some pride in being nominated for this key post. Natal was in trouble; it was over budget and experiencing all the challenges of a multi-campus university. It had four campuses, one in Durban and one in Pietermaritzburg, as well as a medical school and a school of education. Perhaps my experience could be put to service there?

I was appointed at the end of a rigorous interview process. One of the questions I was asked at the interview was how to contain costs in a multi-campus university where the temptation was to duplicate courses and programmes on both the Durban and Pietermaritzburg campuses. I did the best I could at the interview, but, as things turned out, it was this issue that was to make my tenure at the University of Natal unusually short.

At my installation address in September 1991 I said that I was taking office at a 'dangerous time of hope'. South Africa was emerging from one of the most repressive periods in our history. What was the role of the university in this period of reconstruction of our damaged and divided country?

Drawing on my experience of the lay academies in Europe in the mid-1960s, I argued that the university, the academy, 'can in like manner provide the space in which problems of reconstruction [in South Africa] can be addressed'.

But the university itself needed reconstruction. At a time when state subsidies to universities were being cut drastically, Natal, with its four campuses, needed to trim its sails to protect its core business. It was sorely in need of a strategic and organisational review. Should it continue as a multi-campus university? Should it split into a separate university in Pietermaritzburg and another in Durban? What was the future of the medical school?

At my installation I announced that, with the support of the council and the senate, I had instituted a 'Vice Chancellor's Review' (VCR) to 'review our administrative and executive structures', to review our 'elaborate committee system' and to develop 'a comprehensive strategic plan' for the university. The review was to be completed by July 1992.

Bringing about change in a complex organisation such as a university is not a benign process. I became the victim of the process. Who was it who said the most dangerous time in a repressive society is when change has been brought about? Once we began a thorough scrutiny of ourselves, all sorts of structural tensions in the top management of the university became apparent. Coupled with a particularly stormy period of student protests, the fault lines became insurmountable.

After two years of struggle, we were at an impasse. So I sought the views of trusted advisors, on the difficulties I was experiencing with the top team, all of whom I had inherited. The advice I got was:

given the forces at work here you may win some skirmishes, James, even a battle or two, but you won't win the war. It seemed better to cut my losses and leave.

So I entered into negotiations with the chairman of council to leave. I felt that I had failed, that I had been destined to fail because of the inherent unresolved problems.

Can organisations exhibit a 'shadow' side? One of the hallmarks of modern psychotherapy, from Freud and Jung onwards, is its focus on the 'shadow', the dark side of the psyche – those aspects we split off, reject, deny, hide from ourselves, project onto others or disown in some way. Psychotherapists talk about the shadow as the repressed unconscious. It is repressed because we've hidden it from our awareness, and unconscious because we're not aware of it.

As I got to know the university, I became increasingly aware of things repressed that the institution was no longer aware of. The competition for scarce resources between the Durban and Pietermaritzburg campuses led to subterfuge to hide wasteful duplication. There was the dark and contested racist history of the medical school. What of the drop in academic standards as academics marked black scripts by different standards – in the name of 'affirmative action'? And, like other universities, the University of Natal was trapped in apartheid and needed transformation, despite its espousal of the liberal role of an enemy of apartheid in the KwaZulu-Natal region.

The year 1992 was one of protracted student protest action. It started with protests over financial aid. Alarmist headlines in the press fuelled matters. Only careful identification of students without financial aid settled things. We had no sooner resolved that problem when a SRC member, Knowledge Mdlalose, was excluded from the Law Faculty in Durban for poor academic performance and refused to submit himself to a Senate appeal procedure. For two months, the university was the scene of violent student protest, and we had the police on the campus on more than one occasion.

This unprecedented crisis tore the university asunder. In its aftermath, we were confronted by the problem of Nelson Mandela's honorary degree. The ANC in KwaZulu-Natal put pressure on Mr Mandela not to receive his degree at the hand of our Chancellor, Ray Leon, a retired judge. Students protested, carrying placards alleging that Leon was a 'hanging judge', that 'Leon is a murderer'. Inferring that Leon was a supporter of capital punishment. My executive colleagues proposed that we resolve the impasse by persuading our Chancellor to absent himself on the grounds that the university could not guarantee his safety. Having established that Judge Leon had long been opposed to capital punishment and had written extensively on this, I refused. I did not believe that we could take the timorous and time-worn path of least resistance. I called Mr Mandela to inform him that the Chancellor would officiate at the ceremony. Mr Mandela informed me that he had great respect for Ray Leon, who had defended him in the early days of his struggle against the apartheid government, but that he couldn't ignore the will of the ANC. We had a stand-off. As it turned out, Mr Mandela withdrew from the ceremony, citing his busy schedule. In the event, Judge Leon was unable to attend the April graduation ceremony after all. Mr Mandela did finally receive his honorary degree from the university. But by then, Leon had retired and another chancellor had taken office.

In April 1992, there was another incident that illustrates what I was up against. The Chancellor was away and I had to act as chancellor at the graduation ceremony. As I arrived I could hear the sounds of a student protest. Medical students in white coats with stethoscopes swinging from their necks were toyi-toying outside the massive hall where some two thousand people had gathered. The medical students were protesting that some of their number had chosen, for the first time in the history of the university, to participate fully in the graduation. The long, unhappy history of racism in the medical school had ensured that medical students were highly politicised and boycotted most university occasions. On arrival earlier, the Durban campus principal had decided to call on the South African Police to disperse the protestors. After assessing the situation and talking to the student leaders, I took a different view. I was afraid that if the police arrived in force, the protestors would flee into the graduation hall, where the audience was awaiting the start of proceedings. A stampede was possible and many people could be hurt. So I overruled the campus principal, who still insisted that the police should be called.

I negotiated with the protestors to permit three of their number to enter the hall at an appointed time to explain their protest action. Then they would disperse and the ceremony could proceed. The students agreed. So, as Acting Chancellor, I announced this at the start of the ceremony. When the student protestors were invited to speak, the crowd, already tense and anxious, became restive. I sensed that trouble was brewing from the right.

What to do?

I suddenly remembered that Abdullah Ibrahim, South Africa's legendary jazz musician, was to be awarded an honorary doctorate in Music at this ceremony. He was also the main speaker for the night. And I knew that he had composed a piece especially for this occasion. So I sent him a message asking him to play immediately. He quickly summed up the situation, and, as he played the opening bars of his composition, 'Desert Flowers', I felt the temperature dropping. By the time he played the last note, he had the audience in his thrall. Protestors forgotten, the graduation ceremony proceeded without a hitch.

In change-management parlance, I failed at the University of Natal because too many 'well-placed blockers' (John P. Kotter's phrase) in senior positions seemed determined to protect their own interests. My stay as VC was cut short by a deceitful palace revolution that made it impossible for me to give the leadership required to bring about much-needed changes. Deans who have since retired speak with shame of their participation in 'getting rid of Leatt'. They were prey to what sociologist Zigmunt Bauman calls 'moral distantiation'. It's a device used by bureaucracies and organisations to separate the execution of the order from the orderer, so that moral culpability is diffused. The committee of deans, which did not have the full picture, went along with the decision by the few to get rid of me. Implementing decisions to 'downsize' the organisation by retrenching staff, or taking a strike rather than settling with the union, are typical examples of the use of moral distantiation in business and industry.

When the Vice Chancellor's Review team, which comprised senior executives, had completed a draft of their report, by agreement, we asked the British Council to identify a senior university executive from a British multi-campus university. This individual was to provide a constructive critique of the VCR's far-reaching proposals. The registrar of an Irish multi-campus university duly arrived and set to work.

Within a short time, he asked to see me. He cautioned me that if the university was to accept the VCR's proposals, too much power would reside in the campus principals. The centre, including the Office of the Vice Chancellor, would be too weak to provide the requisite leadership and oversight of the university. At the very least, two models needed to be put to the university: one that opted for campus principals, and another in which vice principals had functional rather than campus responsibilities. Instead of robust debate, some of the authors of the report argued that we should not 'listen to our former colonial masters'. They resorted to the old apartheid ploy of criticising the speaker for who he was rather than for the argument made.

Exit James. I could not win this war and left Natal with a heavy heart and a deep sense of opportunity lost. And, I had nowhere to go.

Much of my life has been about taking down walls.

One consistent bright light has been my association with Robinson College, Cambridge. In the late 1980s, I attended a conference on university management at St Catherine's College, Cambridge. One of the speakers was Peter Vaugon, a university registrar. He introduced me to the mysteries of the Oxbridge system and we became firm friends. He nominated me as a Bye Fellow of his college, Robinson. Being a Fellow meant that I could stay at the college and have access to the resources of the university. I spent a number of weeks at Robinson College in subsequent years digging into the wonderful library system, thinking, reflecting – and healing.

When things fall apart, the future looks bleak. Was I washed up, at fifty-four? Would anyone again entrust me with responsibility? In those dark days I learned first-hand what Buddhists mean when they say you have to make room for the experience of failure, the grief, the misery, the not knowing. You don't know whether this is the end of the story. It may be the beginning of a new one.

Jenny, ever supportive, and I moved back into our Rondebosch home in Cape Town. I cooled my heels for months, with little to do and no real prospects. I did take up a sport I'd not done for years: horse riding. I owned and kept a horse in Noordhoek. Riding in the crisp morning air, when Bellah was fresh after a good night's rest, was magical. Sadly she died. After that, I rented a beautiful white horse called Frodo, which I rode near the Tokai forest. What a pleasure.

In 1994, a momentous year for the country, the first democratic elections were held, on 27 April. Few will forget the long queues of South Africans, black and white, waiting patiently to cast their votes. On 10 May, Nelson Mandela was inaugurated the first President of a democratic South Africa.

Sometime in that momentous year I received a call from Wieland Gevers, Deputy Vice Chancellor at UCT, asking me to help establish an academic consortium in the Western Cape. I jumped at the opportunity. It was to be a six-month commission to create the infrastructure for what came to be known as the Cape Higher Education Consortium (CHEC). The Universities of Cape Town, Stellenbosch and the Western Cape, as well as the Cape and Peninsula Technikons, were to form the consortium to accomplish jointly what they could not accomplish as individual institutions.

Universities were having to do more with less as state funding decreased and South Africa's 'massification' of higher education got under way. What was of concern was the state of the libraries in the CHEC institutions. Years of academic boycott and limited funding had emptied shelves. Moreover, the University of the Western Cape and Peninsula Technikon, created by the apartheid government, had inadequate libraries.

What was needed was an innovative, systemic approach. And it came with an offer from the Ford Foundation to finance an investigation into what it would take to create a library consortium using the latest available library information software. The investigation showed that a 'library without walls' was possible. The technology was available to create a shared library information system to give the 70 000 students and staff, from all five institutions, identical access to all parts of the existing, and unevenly endowed, libraries. The institutions were no more than forty kilometres apart and the political will existed. Thus, the first major project of CHEC was born. And I soon found myself appointed as chief executive officer of the consortium, a contract that was to last for eleven years.

Major funding from overseas donors made possible the Cape Library Co-operative, or CALICO as it is known to this day. All the libraries were linked to a single state-of-the-art library information software system. A daily shuttle service moved books and periodicals between libraries and, as modern communication technology developed, resources were shared online. As we said at the time,

CALICO was the result of a hard-won fit between vision, technology and organisation.

Imagine being able to enter one of the libraries, say at UWC, log on to the network and access the library holdings of UCT and Stellenbosch yourself. Imagine, further, requesting a book or journal from one of these libraries with the understanding that within a short time the article would be in your hands, delivered by shuttle. Imagine that. A library without walls – more than twenty years ago.

A key to the success of this library consortium, the first in the country, was finding a solution to the high cost of bandwidth in South Africa. Bandwidth was prohibitively expensive and the government-owned national telecommunications company, Telkom, had a monopoly. After much effort, including pressure from the presidents of US donor organisations on the top Telkom executives, a contract was signed between higher education institutions and Telkom for cheaper national and international bandwidth.

The universities and technikons created a first for South Africa. A not-for-profit company, called Tertiary Education Network or TENET. As a founder member of the TENET board, I am proud of what has been achieved to make bandwidth accessible to teachers and researchers. And the bandwidth played on, you might say. Today, TENET manages sophisticated services in research networking that match the best in the world. It is acknowledged as one of the outstanding equity projects in South African higher education.

The CHEC library consortium was proof that infrastructural collaboration between competing institutions was possible. What about academic collaboration? Given the history of government interference in universities, the five higher education institutions in the Western Cape were jealous of their independence. Each had its particular history and values. Strange bedfellows. One was liberal, another steeped in Afrikaner history, two were creatures of apartheid separate development policy, and one was the product of the deep divide between theory and practice evident in our higher education policy history.

Was it possible to build a platform across these 'silos', so that academic teaching and research could be planned more systemically, and more responsively? This question became more pressing when the Minister of Education appointed a National Working Group (NWG) to restructure higher education and eradicate the footprint of apartheid. The NWG eventually chose mergers as the chief means of carrying out its mandate.

The CHEC institutions took the view that none of them should be merged. They argued instead for a 'systemic approach' to higher education in the Western Cape. With the support of donors, a powerful argument was developed for creating systemic platforms across the silos to enable a more rational approach to teaching and research that was also more responsive to regional and national needs. In other words, to borrow from game theory, we said that competing institutions can 'co-operate' under certain conditions and within agreed 'rules of the game'.

Ultimately, our advice was ignored and the Cape and Peninsula technikons were merged to form the Cape Peninsula University of Technology. We took our submission to heart and created an innovative platform for nursing education that spanned all our institutions. And we did this without the necessary incentives from government. 'Co-opetition' is a neologism that describes the way competing organisations can, at the same time, co-operate with one another. Co-opetition is possible, even for universities that jealously guard their autonomy. But we found that it is hard work when it is entirely self-generated, when the leaders have to agree to co-operate for the long-term good of society.

Co-opetition was given fresh impetus when we focused on the development needs of the region. Universities worldwide were undergoing seismic changes as they grappled with the advent of the knowledge economy and rising expectations from society. Twenty-first-century universities could no longer afford to be ivory towers (if ever they had been). Perpetuating the life of scholarship for its own sake was no longer possible. The world depended increasingly on universities for knowledge and policy-thinking. *Engagement* with society had become an imperative of the university's mission.

For the first time in our history, we had a popularly elected government willing to tap into the resources of all the country's universities. And this was certainly the case in the Western Cape. The strategic development goals of provincial government could only be achieved with the help of the universities. A historic compact between the provincial government and the CHEC institutions became possible. In preparing for this, the provincial government laid out its strategies for sectoral development, and the CHEC institutions completed an audit of their undergraduate and postgraduate courses and research activities. The compact committed both parties to align their work wherever possible. Engagement thus became the new imperative to drive co-opetition.

The stage was set for CHEC to develop in new directions. By this time (2005), I was nearing my mid-sixties and beginning to think about retirement when I received a call for help from an unlikely quarter. My life seems to have followed these calls and callings.

The call was from Allyson Lawless, on behalf of the Chair of the Council of the University of Venda (Univen), South Africa's northernmost university. The university needed an acting vice chancellor for six months. I learned that the Council had had to deal firmly with the complex leadership problems at the university by placing the vice chancellor and deputy vice chancellor on extended leave, pending the appointment of a new vice chancellor.

After consulting the CHEC leadership, Jenny and I agreed to assist. The agreement all round was that I would continue as CEO of CHEC part-time and spend about ten days at Univen each month. Univen would appoint the acting registrar to work with me as part of an Interim Management Team. Our mandate was to ensure the smooth running of the university while the recruitment of a new VC went on. I remember the dilapidated state of the campus when we arrived, the look of expectancy on the faces of the people and my feeling of nervous exhilaration. Daunting challenges faced us, many miles from home, holed up in a nondescript hotel room. It's hard to imagine the almost insurmountable odds facing the average student of a rural university such as Univen. Mashudu Dakalo came to Univen having come top of his class in the rural hinterland of Limpopo province, but with a matric pass that only just qualified him for admission. One of his enduring problems was the English language, the medium of instruction at Univen. English was not a second language for Mashudu; it was a *foreign* tongue. He had trouble understanding English, let alone speaking it. But he had persevered and was in his final year of a social science degree when I met him as a student leader on campus. He was bright, intelligent and knew that Univen needed help if it was going to survive. He gave me strong support during my term there.

Some months before I was appointed, Jonathan Jansen, then Dean of Education at the University of Pretoria who became Vice Chancellor of the University of the Free State, was invited to speak on the Univen campus. He reported later that when he saw the poor state of the campus and was able to gauge the low morale of students and staff he changed his talk somewhat. He asked the question, 'When does a university cease to be a university?'

103

After one month in office, I had the answer. A university ceases to be a university when the infrastructure can no longer support its core business of teaching and research. I was appalled at what I discovered. The Council was completely out of touch with what was happening on this rural campus, a five-hour drive from Johannesburg, because it conducted its quarterly meetings in Johannesburg. The university residences, teaching and research facilities, library and administrative offices were run-down. The campus, originally built for five thousand students, comprised some thirteen thousand enrolled students. The water supply was inadequate, electricity shortages were frequent and there was little evidence of waste management. The campus was dirty and unkempt. There were simply no computer facilities for students and few for staff. The student hostels could accommodate just over one and a half thousand students, but on any given night three times that number squatted in the hostels. Students cooked on hotplates in their rooms because there were no dining facilities. Their wet waste was disposed of in the ablutions, resulting in blocked toilets. The list of infrastructural problems seemed endless. Morale was low. This was emphatically not a six-month holding job.

We sought an urgent meeting with the Minister of Education, Naledi Pandor. I argued that Univen was a disgrace as a public university. If Univen had a place in the government's long-term thinking, then it needed serious urgent funding. 'If not, close it,' I suggested. The Minister responded that Univen was part of government's long-term thinking. She asked for a plan and an estimate of what it would take to deal with the problems.

We set about drawing up a plan for Univen's turnaround and in a relatively short time had the Minister's support for a major cash injection for a 'recovery plan'. After three years of hard work by all concerned and nearly half a billion rand of government funding, Univen was well on the road to recovery.

The plan comprised four legs. The first leg dealt with infrastructural renewal. We used professional project managers to assist us. Buildings were renovated and hostels renewed. Information and communications infrastructure and services were developed. All this on a live campus. By the time I left, all students had email addresses and had access to computers.

The second leg of recovery dealt with the core business of teaching and learning. We began the process of converting the university into a 'comprehensive' university in terms of the government's mandate. This meant introducing student enrolment planning to get control of student admissions. We reviewed academic programme offerings to cut out wasteful duplication. We began the process of gearing up for the teaching and learning challenges facing a rural university that drew students who were severely underprepared because of the school system.

The third leg of the recovery was called new campus development. We entered into a compact with government that set student enrolment at ten thousand. This meant that we had to increase classroom space and utilise space more effectively. We also needed to increase the number of beds in our hostels and to feed the students.

The fourth leg dealt with management and organisational problems. Essentially, Univen needed to learn to do the basics right when it came to management. We introduced performance management. We dealt with the bloated top structure of the organisation. We put in place an internal audit. We updated human resources policies and practices. We undertook a review of financial controls and procurement practices.

By the time I left Univen in 2008, the campus buildings were sparkling. I walked around the campus one last time. Now, students had access to computer labs. There were toilets in the lecture block where there had been none. I was particularly pleased with the newly renovated hostels. I love it when a plan comes together, I thought to myself. The newly appointed vice chancellor was in place. My mandate was done. And the Council's decisive interventions were hailed as exemplary.

The time had come for me to retire.

I have been involved at executive management level in three universities undergoing major transitions: Cape Town, Natal and Venda. In fact, during my career the whole university system had undergone massive changes.

UCT experienced its own version of what the literature calls the massification of higher education. This occurs when, for various reasons, the doors of learning are opened to those who hitherto had little or no access. In Great Britain, this happened with the advent of the 'redbrick' universities, when social class became less of an impediment to access. UCT was, in effect, the cause of its own massification when it decided to open its doors of learning and halls of residence to all races, under the leadership of Dr Stuart Saunders in the 1980s. For the first time, African, Coloured and Indian students were admitted to study at UCT and live in its residences, despite the restrictive laws prohibiting this. And, like all experiences of massification, UCT had to manage the expectations of newcomers and the reticence of its traditional base. A raft of new issues had to be confronted. Race relations and racial conflict had to be managed, particularly in our halls of residence. Black students admitted to UCT generally came woefully underprepared for university study; academic support programmes had to be crafted to assist them to realise their potential without lowering standards. Black students generally came from poor homes; student funding mechanisms had to be invented to enable students to pay their way. The challenges were daunting.

Universities worldwide did not routinely engage in strategic planning when I appointed the Vice Chancellor's Review at the University of Natal in 1991. Certainly Natal had not done so. The university was over budget and growing apace with a great deal of wasteful duplication of academic and support programmes. The purpose of the review was to contain costs and rationalise operations wherever possible. The mandate of the review team was wide, and we sought the assistance of internationally experienced consultants. What I learned from the Natal experience is that voluntary change, change that is initiated by the university itself, is neither benign nor easy to implement. Vested interests are strong and resistance to change is easy to underestimate. In the final analysis, some of the changes I had envisaged but could not effect were forced upon the university when government restructured higher education in the late 1990s. The University of Natal and the University of Durban-Westville were merged to form one of the largest contact universities in South Africa.

At the time I was appointed acting VC of the University of Venda, in 2005, the crisis faced by that university was truly life-threatening. Years of neglect on the part of senior management and an absentee governing council had resulted in the degradation and demoralisation of the campus. Only a massive turnaround strategy, driven by a newly invigorated council, and materially supported by government, could possibly succeed. Rural universities the world over are at a severe disadvantage; it is difficult to attract and retain good staff, and student accommodation on campus is an expensive requisite. And, in the nature of things, the rural university is usually the largest employer in the region, with the resultant labour relations problems. Such institutions are strategically important for regional development, but they require special handling. This is something we have been slow to learn in South Africa.

Looking east

The heart has reasons that reason cannot know.
  – Pascal

Perplext in faith, but pure in deeds,
  At last he beat his music out.
There lives more faith in honest doubt,
  Believe me, than in half the creeds.
  – Tennyson, 'In Memoriam'

Looking back over my autobiographical *Interludes*, there is no doubt that several different people had been involved in this exercise of retrieval, all of whom are named James Leatt, and assembled differently somehow with each passing phase. Catherine Malabou's trenchant observation comes to mind: 'The work proper to the brain that engages with history and individual experience has a name: *plasticity*.'

While in the preceding chapters I've engaged with history and experience, in the following, I want to concentrate on the cognitive road map I've been developing to help me make sense of where I am and who I am and to explore further the reciprocity between my personal journey and my philosophical reflections.

Rudyard Kipling claimed that East and West could never meet. And, judging from my school and university education, he was right. We seldom looked eastward, and when we did, it was usually in an unsympathetic way. Things Eastern were treated as strange, inscrutable, even esoteric and unintelligible. But thankfully paradigms have been changing.

I understood the extent of my ignorance when in the mid-1970s I began teaching in the Department of Religious Studies at UCT, where Hinduism and Buddhism formed part of the curriculum. I treasure those early years of intellectual exploration and discovery when I played catch-up. Yet, it was only much later that I encountered the actual practice of meditation and began to get the hang of a different take on the world. By this time I was no longer comfortable within the Western monotheistic family of religions, and I had also come to see the limitations of what we have been calling a Western science-based rationality.

I am a proud heir to a tradition that goes back 2 500 years to early Greek philosophers, such as Socrates and Plato. It places a premium on reason, calculation, planning – in short, on the means-ends rationality that has given us science, technology and modern administrative systems. It gave us the Enlightenment, with its emphasis on the authority of reason rather than religion. It has given us Einstein and Hawking. It is the source of modern medicine, of startling reductions in infant mortality, and of unprecedented longevity. The fruits of this development led John F. Kennedy to say in the 1960s that for the first time in human history we have the means to feed everyone (even if the will is absent). We also have the technology literally to kill the world.

And it's worth recalling that early Greek philosophy also emphasised spirituality and spiritual practice – nothing to do with gods – a 'secular spirituality', if you will. I don't believe science can fully explain the world. I know that 'the heart has reasons that reason cannot know', as Blaise Pascal memorably said. He was talking about the age-old conflict between Christian faith and reason. I, who no longer find Christianity compelling, use the sentence in a different sense. The new 'language' I sought had to be one that helped me make sense of spirituality in a secular world, to create and understand my own reality.

I found elements of this new language in another tradition, this time from the East, from Asia, which also goes back some 2 500 years. This tradition has concentrated on what might be called 'contemplative thinking'. On understanding human consciousness, on training and disciplining the mind. It includes the millennia-old Buddhist, Zen and Taoist traditions of meditation practice. I am not a card-carrying member of any Buddhist group, though I have meditated for years. And a glance at my bookshelf friends will confirm this.

This is the tradition that trains the mind to 'scent' – in the old sense of 'divine', or sense something – before thought or thinking. It trains the mind to be conscious, awakened, mindful. Zen practice deliberately seeks to discombobulate or disturb the comfort of reason. It challenges you be open to 'reasons of the heart'. I think 'contemplative thinking' is what the artist or composer is engaged in when waiting upon the creative muse.

In the West, we usually distinguish between philosophy and religion. Religion is generally understood to embrace the three monotheistic religions with their belief in a radically transcendent, Supreme Being: Yahweh, God or Allah. Philosophy is the study of the general and abstract features of the world and the categories with which we think, such as mind, matter, reason, proof, truth, etc.

I can no longer accept Judaism, Christianity and Islam's appropriation of the word 'religion'. Nor can I accept the appropriation of the word 'philosophy' by the West to the exclusion of what we can learn from the East.

What happens if you try to work at the intersection between West and East?

One way into this is to think about the use of *doubt* proposed by the great Western philosopher René Descartes, and what Buddhism calls 'great doubt'.

One of the features of modernity is the break with the authority of the elders in whatever form. Descartes is called the father of modern philosophy because, in the seventeenth century, he was bold enough to ask whether we can be certain of anything outside of the tradition and the teaching of the elders. In his famous statement, *Cogito ergo sum* (I think therefore I am), he believed he had established such a foundation for truth in reason. What Descartes was anxious to attempt was a fixed and stable, perhaps even absolute, foundation for knowledge. The only other possibility seemed to be nihilism, where nothing is certain.

We now understand better the errors of such attempts to find the one sure and certain foundation for truth beyond doubt. And, if the truth be told, we are still trying to overcome the dichotomies that can be traced back to Descartes. Dichotomies, such as body/soul, mind/matter and good/evil.

But these same dichotomies have led to the predominance of instrumental and utilitarian cost-benefit thinking, which, in turn, have led to the exploitation of nature. We lack ecological intelligence, for instance. We are in danger of ecological collapse because we deplete natural resources while polluting the environment with toxic waste. We may be losing our fight against global warming because of our addiction to growth and consumerism. Our pitting of humans against nature has put us on a suicidal path.

Eastern thought has confronted the human need for secure foundations. It stands on its head our tendency to reach for absolute truth and to fear nihilism. Absolutism and nihilism arise out of our attempts to find certainty and a stable sense of the self. When we learn to live with the questions and embrace groundlessness, we experience a measure of freedom. We are no longer hostage to certainty or the lack thereof.

Zen Buddhism encourages great doubt. We are inspired to push our doubts (What am I? Why do I exist?) to their very limits as conscious acts of the doubting self. The thirteenth-century Buddhist thinker Dogen put it simply:

> The way of the Buddha is to know yourself;
> To know yourself is to forget yourself;
> To forget yourself is to be awakened by all things.

Mindful awareness, a Buddhist would say, takes you beyond the conceptual, beyond belief, where the mind has nowhere to rest, where the questioning is within the unknowing self. This questioning is different from conventional inquiry; it has no interest in finding an answer. It starts at the point where descriptions and explanations end. The deeper we penetrate the mystery, the more the mystery deepens.

'Great doubt' is a function of contemplative thinking as opposed to the calculative thinking of a Descartes. Zen Buddhists may not believe in God, but they are interested in the ultimate questions that 'great doubt' uncovers – fundamental questions about the meaning of life and death, and about pain and suffering. But they approach them differently.

The task of establishing how you know something to be the case is called epistemology. Here's Cathcart's and Klein's humorous take:

> DIMITRI: *I'm feeling good now, Tasso. I've got logic down cold, so the rest should be a picnic in the Acropolis.*
> TASSO: *What Acropolis?*
> DIMITRI: *That one! Right over there! Maybe you need to ease off on the ouzo, pal.*
> TASSO: *But is that the Acropolis or just something that you believe is the Acropolis? How do you know it's real? For that matter, how do you know anything is real?*
> DIMITRI: *Next round's on me.*

I first encountered the challenge of epistemology during my undergraduate years at Rhodes University. How do you know that a claim like 'God exists' is true? Or what would it take to falsify such a claim?

Antony Flew famously dealt with the question by telling a parable. Once upon a time, two explorers came upon a clearing in the jungle.

Many flowers and many weeds were growing in the clearing. One of the explorers says, 'Some gardener must tend this plot.' The other disagrees: 'There is no gardener.' So they pitch their tents and set a watch. No gardener is ever seen. 'But perhaps he is an invisible gardener.' So they set up a barbed-wire fence, they electrify it, and they patrol with bloodhounds. Nothing. Yet still, the Believer is not convinced. 'But there is a gardener, invisible, intangible, insensible to electric shocks, who leaves no scent and makes no sound, a gardener who comes secretly ...' Finally the Sceptic despairs: 'But what remains of your original assertion? Just how does what you call an invisible, intangible, eternally elusive gardener differ from an imaginary gardener or even from no gardener at all?'

This parable challenged my taken-for-granted world. I have since learned to question previously held assumptions, to feel comfortable with ambiguity, irony, paradox and uncertainty. In short, I learned the value of the dynamics of *doubt*. At the feet of many teachers, at Rhodes and after, I learned that dogmatic belief closes off questions, that the security of a belief system is that you are no longer troubled by the original questioning.

Any ideology, religious or secular, is just that: a lens. An interpretation of reality, a way of knowing. An action-system that, in the case of Afrikaner Nationalism, for example, prescribes the way you organise society and the political economy.

I well remember Daantjie Oosthuizen, our beloved philosophy professor at Rhodes, drawing a framed picture of a cat on the board. 'The cat fills the whole picture for someone trapped in an ideology,' said the Prof. They can't see that their perspective is framed, enclosed, blinkered. Then he proceeded to rub out the frame until all that was left was the cat. 'No one mistakes a cat for the whole truth,' he offered.

A religious belief system can be described as a 'total ideology', an all-embracing answer to our deepest questionings. It makes the profound claim for itself that *one* view of the world, namely, its view, is *the* view of the world – an example of Niebuhr's 'scandal of particularity', by the way.

At Rhodes, I was pushed off this comfortable perch and had to learn to fly. And over the years, I suppose I have developed the trust to doubt, to test the truth of any totalising claim against the wings of experience.

In the brand of Christianity I grew up with, doubt was a dirty word. I have come to understand that doubt is not a psychological defect, an interruption in the normal development of a person. It is a normal state of perplexity. All the truly Big Questions – about life and death, pain and suffering, body and mind, about the meaning of it all – are not resolved by adopting one or other belief system. Perplexity is the very place within us where awakening is closest. Such doubt beats at the heart of a spiritual crisis. When we can no longer accept without questioning the tenets of our religious traditions, we need the courage to doubt. Allow your questions to arise and follow them honestly. Here is how the Sufi poet and mystic Rumi puts it:

> I have lived on the lip
> Of insanity, wanting to know the reasons,
> Knocking on the door. It opens.
> I've been knocking from the inside!

Perhaps this is why Zen Buddhism holds so much appeal for some Westerners. You could say Zen Buddhism enables us to develop our sense of mystery through contemplative thinking, non-thinking and questioning. And it has been this way for many centuries. What Zen is saying is that when it comes to the Big Questions, when it comes to the mystery of life and death, you need to unlearn the language of calculation and learn anew the language of contemplative thinking. The answer to the mystery is not to be found at the end of a rational argument, a mathematical formula, a telescope or a microscope. The mystery of life is a lived experience.

Martin Heidegger first introduced a distinction between calculative and meditative thinking. The Engen service station in the main road in my town is an example of calculative thinking. The petrol and diesel fuels sold there are extracted from non-renewable fossils by complex chemical engineering processes. The business plan used by the owner to manage his business is based on means-end calculations. The trade union that represents the petrol attendants is organised along rational lines. Writing in 1955, Heidegger felt that calculative thinking is insatiable. 'Nature,' he laments, 'becomes a giant gasoline station, an energy source for modern technology and industry ...'

You're engaged in meditative thinking when you think about means/end reasoning. It is the thinking we use when we are thinking about thinking. When we are reflecting on the meaning of things. Heidegger illustrates meditative or contemplative thinking in this way.

At an international meeting of Nobel Prize winners in 1955, an American chemist boldly claimed: 'The hour is near when life will be placed in the hands of the chemist who will be able to synthesise, split and change living substance at will.' We 'marvel at the daring of scientific research, without thinking about it', says Heidegger. This is scientism at its worst. Unreflective and arrogant. Surely the fact that we can do something does not mean that we ought to do it. What was the man thinking?

As Stephen Batchelor says of meditation or meditative thinking (*Verses from the Center: A Buddhist Vision of the Sublime*, 2008):

> Meditation does not add anything to life; it recovers what has been lost. It is a growing awareness of what our existence is saying to and asking of us ... Meditation and mystery are inseparable. The core of a meditative attitude is questioning itself. Such questioning, though, has nothing to do with the curiosity of calculation. For meditative questioning partakes

in the nature of the mystery itself. It is a kind of fundamental astonishment or perplexity.

And in learning this new language of meditative thinking, there are aids, which I will share elsewhere in this book.

A premise of rationality: you cannot simply accept something as the truth because God said it, or because it is in the Bible, or because some authority has asserted it.

When I discovered Reinhold Niebuhr (1892 - 1971) in the early 1970s, I encountered a Protestant theologian who understood that truth claims have to be tested against experience. Niebuhr spent considerable intellectual energy trying to persuade people that there is a match between faith and politics, between the truth claims of Christianity and political realities. He lamented that many could accept his political views but not the presuppositions upon which they were built. Presuppositions which, in Niebuhr's case, were built on his liberal, Protestant Christian faith. He stood in the William James tradition as both an empiricist and a religious man whose faith was both the consequence and the presupposition of his pragmatism.

Niebuhr invoked colourful metaphors. He likened religion and science to portrait painting and portrait photography, respectively. Like portrait photography, science tells many little truths in the interests of the great lie. Religion tells many little lies in the interests of a great truth. The great lie is that everything can be reduced to science; questions about meaning have no place. The great truth is that questions about the meaning of it all can only be expressed in myth and metaphor, and not in science.

On what he called the 'circular relation between truth and experience', Niebuhr used the analogy of spectacles. When your spectacles enable you to navigate the physical world you are okay. But when you find that you keep bumping into things you don't say they shouldn't be there. You go to the optometrist. I summarised

Niebuhr's position this way: the presuppositions of faith act as a filter ... like spectacles without which we cannot see. But, if evidence other than your sight leads you to believe your spectacles are inadequate, you will change them. In my doctoral dissertation, I developed the notion of 'adequation'. It's an inelegant word but it does help to express the relationship between truth and experience. In any organised religion there is what might be called 'truth *within* a tradition'. If you accept the basic tenets of theism, for example, many of the claims of Judaism, Islam and Christianity will hold true for you. There is coherence or logic to the discourse of these monotheistic religions. And the discourse of monotheism will hold true for you until something happens to cause you to question fundamentally the truth *of* that tradition.

'Adequation' happens when there is a fit between what you believe, the specs you wear, and the world you experience. But what happens when the truth *within* the tradition no longer holds, when you doubt the truth *of* the tradition. What is the tipping point, what needs to happen, for adequation to fail? For me it was the Holocaust. Slowly but inexorably, my reading and thinking about the Holocaust led me to call into question my fondly held belief in the almighty, all-present, all-knowing, loving God of theism. There was no longer 'adequation' between my faith and the world of my experience.

The Holocaust is a pre-eminent test of faith. The question persists, after Belsen, Dachau, Auschwitz what is the meaning of good, of God?

The closest I have gotten to an answer is the aforementioned work of Hans Jonas. After the war, Jonas worked on what he called 'a search for Good after Auschwitz'. His is a searingly honest attempt to grapple with these issues in what is called 'post-holocaust theology'.

In a lecture he delivered in 1984 on receiving the Leopold Lucas Prize at Tübingen University, Jonas offered a piece of speculative theology entitled 'The Concept of God after Auschwitz: A Jewish Voice'. In a deeply personal grappling, Jonas told a myth about a *suffering*, *becoming* and *caring* God who, from the beginning of time, gave himself over unreservedly to an 'unconditional immanence' and divested himself of his deity and foreknowledge of how the world would turn out, especially after the evolution of human beings.

This myth of God's *self*-limitation, argues Jonas, enables him to dispense with the (medieval) notion of omnipotence beloved of Judaic teaching. It enables him to argue with the Jewish Kabbalah for 'God's self-limitation' in which 'divine fate is bound up with the coming-to-be of a world'. This radical self-limitation means, even, that God cannot be said to have foreseen the possibility of an Auschwitz any more than he could have foreseen an Ette Hillesum, the Dutch Jew who *volunteered* for work in a concentration camp and was murdered in Auschwitz. God's 'chosen voidance' was made so that we could be, exist – without the threat or promise of divine intervention.

Jonas's answer to the age-old question of theodicy is: if, after Auschwitz, you cannot give up the concept of God, then at least you will have to give up any notion of God as the 'Lord of History' and settle for God suffering with us in this world. Not something most Jews, Muslims or Christians could readily assent to.

Auschwitz, as a symbol of man's inhumanity to man, has been hardwired into my brain. Auschwitz represents the shadow side of modernity, the conscious and deliberate use of bureaucracy and technology to exterminate millions of people. And although I'd served as a Methodist minister for sixteen years, the problem of theodicy had dogged my journey and I had to face the crisis of faith growing in me.

Either there is a God or there isn't. I agree with Adi Ophir: 'If there is a God it is necessary to explain why a world that could have been less evil is replete with (evil) … we are left with only three possible answers: either God isn't omnipotent, or there are limits to his goodness or both … It is even possible to restore all his potency or all his goodness. But it is impossible to restore both.' Hans Jonas's notion of a suffering God is an example of a theodicy which limits God's omnipotence, but none that I know of limit his unbounded goodness. The post-modern philosophers who wish to speak of God try to get around the problem by speaking of a God who 'emptied himself' of his power in order to identify with suffering humanity. But I can no longer subscribe to the concept of God after the Holocaust.

Either way, it seems that we human beings are on our own in the face of the evil for which we are responsible, on our own to face the evil that we can prevent or at least reduce.

I would argue that conversion from one religion or ideology to another occurs when adequation fails, when there is no longer a fit between what you believe and your world of experience. Confirmation of this failure of fit comes from, of all things, marketing theory. What does it take for a person to 'convert' from a position held with conviction to something else? My colleague, Jan Hofmeyr, believed that people 'bring a complex range of needs, desires and values to every decision that they make'. No matter what you are choosing, be it a job, a car or a religious commitment, you tend to become attached to it if it works for you. There is a 'needs-values fit and commitment'. People often stick to their choice of job, car or religion even when it makes them unhappy, so it seems. And the greater your commitment to your job, car or religion, the more you are willing to tolerate dissatisfaction. This is a measure of your involvement.

Religion matters to many people. It provides justifications for such mysteries as suffering and pain; it inspires by offering salvation in this life and heaven in a life to come. It consoles when you are facing suffering and death; and it provides a community for the like-minded.

What is the straw that breaks the camel's back when it comes to your job, car or your religion? What happens when there is no longer a fit between your needs and values, between your experience and your beliefs? 'Cognitive dissonance' is what the psychologists call it. We start feeling ambivalent and uncertain, our commitment and involvement weakens. The alternatives start to look attractive – we 'convert' from one job or brand of car to another. We find we can no longer subscribe to the tenets of our religion; it no longer meets our complex web of needs and values.

But you don't have to convert. Instead of swapping one set of ideological beliefs for another, you can decide to be agnostic about such overarching belief systems. The great English biologist T. H. Huxley invented the term 'agnosticism' in 1869 to describe a rigorous approach, or a method, for dealing with Big Questions. Put positively, this means: 'Follow your reason as far as it will take you.' Expressed negatively, Huxley's principle of agnosticism says: 'Do not pretend that conclusions are certain which are not demonstrated or demonstrable.' This principle of agnosticism runs through the Western tradition, from Socrates to modern science. It's also the key to understanding the teaching of Siddhartha Gautama, also known as the Buddha.

There is a moment in the life of Siddhartha Gautama when he is passing through the village of Kesaputta in India, where the Kalamas lived. They ask him for advice on what to do about the many holy men who come to the village expounding their teachings and criticising others. How can they tell which teaching to follow? The Buddha responds that they must test the truth claims of the holy men against their experience. Listen to what the holy men are saying but question and test the teachings. 'Do not be satisfied with hearsay or with tradition or with legendary lore or with what has come down in the scriptures or with conjecture or with logical inference or with weighing evidence or with liking for a view after pondering over it or with someone else's ability ...'

How then will they know? The Buddha replies, 'When you know in yourselves: "These things are wholesome, blameless, commended by the wise, and being adopted and put into effect they lead to welfare and happiness", then you should practise and abide in them ...'

Don't accept some truth-claim as gospel. *Test it.* Siddhartha Gautama's teaching is not about yet another -ism to believe in, it is something to be *done*. He challenged people to understand the nature of anguish and its origins. He taught that anguish can be overcome, that it is possible to liberate yourself. Once, when asked what he was doing, the Buddha replied that he taught 'anguish and the ending of anguish'. When he was asked about metaphysics – the origin and end of the universe, the identity or difference of body and mind, his existence or non-existence after death (the Big Questions) – he remained silent.

Don't take my word for it, says Siddhartha Gautama. Ask yourselves, does this truth-claim enable us to live well? That is the question.

There are many helpful introductory books on Buddhism and Taoism; some are listed in the Bibliography at the end of this book. What I want to do here is to indicate some of the liberating insights that have helped me on my journey.

One of my early discoveries was the typically Eastern or Asian notion of 'non-dualism'. I don't know about you, but I was brought up on a diet of dualisms – body/mind, us/them, spirit/matter, me/you, good/evil, sacred/secular, either/or – the list is endless. Indeed, in order to describe who we are, we tend to draw a mental boundary line; everything *inside* the boundary is me, my 'self', and everything *outside* the boundary is 'not-me', 'not-self'. Our most obvious boundary is the skin.

Do I feel I *am* a body or that I *have* a body? Most of us would say we have a body – as though it was something we own, like a car or a cellphone. But, in fact I am my body. The dualism here is troublesome. Watch a professional tennis player, like Andy Murray, at odds with his game. He behaves like someone who has a forehand that is not obeying his instructions, as though it was out there and not part of who he is. Worse still, he smashes his racket on the ground as though the racket too is at fault.

There's a wonderful line by James Joyce in *Dubliners* that sums it up. 'Mr Duffy lived a short distance from his body.' As though he could. And, of course, boundary lines are potential battle lines; lines of conflict are marked out. Ken Wilber suggests that every time we draw a boundary we create a potential battle zone. That's when we attempt to strike out one of the opposites. Take the opposites of life versus death; when we are young we attempt to eradicate death from our thinking and living. That's why Buddhist meditation practice encourages one to meditate on death, to visualise a decaying corpse, so that death is made part of life.

The essential insight I took from the East is that however vivid the differences between opposites may be – life/death, body/soul, good/evil – they are nevertheless 'completely inseparable and mutually interdependent, and for the simple reason that the one could not live without the other. Looked at in this way, there is obviously no inside without an outside, no up without down, no win without loss, no pleasure without pain, no life without death.' Vintage Ken Wilber.

My favourite translation of and commentary on the *Dao De Jing* (also known as the *Tao Te Ching*, the basis of Taoism), by Roger Ames and David Hall, describes the 'mutuality of opposites' in Taoism in this way: 'Young is "young-becoming-old"; dark is "dark-becoming-light"; soft is "soft-becoming-hard". In the fullness of time, any and all of the qualities that define each event will yield themselves up to their opposites.' The unity of opposites, or the practice of consciously living without boundaries, is not an idea confined to Eastern, or Western, mystics. Modern-day physics attests to the unity of opposites. As Wilber says, relativity theory holds that rest versus motion are totally indistinguishable – 'each is both'. It is no longer possible to separate time and motion. In short, boundary lines are never found in the real world itself, but only in the imagination of the mapmakers. It's like the old woman on her first international flight. Looking down she exclaims, 'There are no borders.'

What difference does it make to try to think and live non-dualistically, in a world without boundaries? Well, for a start I begin to realise that all boundaries are constructs. They can be redrawn, erased, deconstructed. I am no longer a casualty of what Alfred North Whitehead called 'the fallacy of misplaced concreteness' – the fallacy that because someone has drawn a line, a boundary to demarcate opposites, I need to observe the boundary as though it were real. It is hugely liberating not to be hostage to the boundary between sacred and secular, between English and Afrikaner, between male and female, between black and white ...

Boundaries are illusory, says Wilber. The East never really fell into the fallacy of confusing the map with the territory, boundaries with reality, symbols with actuality, names with what is named ... Hence, when Buddhists say reality is void, they mean it is void of boundaries ... The point is that when the world is seen to be void of boundaries then all things and all events – just like all opposites – are seen to be mutually dependent and interpenetrating.

This is difficult to accept because we cling to our boundaries as if our lives depended on them. What I learned from Eastern spirituality is that all our boundaries are constructs – useful fictions. They are not where the battle lines need to be drawn. As Wilber says, 'Thus the battle is not solved, but dissolved.'

When I started exploring modern Buddhist thought and practice, I soon came across the notion of 'no-self' ('not-self' or 'nonself'). Like most Westerners, I found it discombobulating, disconcerting and disturbing. Is Buddhism saying that the self is an illusion? Why is this notion of the self so unnerving?

I suppose it is because we seem to spend our lives shoring up and defending our sense of self, warding off challenges to our 'ego-self', the sense that 'I am a VIP, a very important person' – my egoism or self-centeredness. Perhaps our fixed sense of the self, like vestiges of original sin, remains with us long after we have ceased to believe in it? But surely I need a strong sense of self if I am to mature as a person – a healthy selfhood, if you like? The Buddhist notion of 'no-self' seems to be directed at the ego-self. To unpack this in a manner I could grasp, I had to await the publication of Stephen Batchelor's study of the second-century Buddhist philosopher-monk, Nagarjuna: *Verses from the Center: A Buddhist Vision of the Sublime* (2008).

At the heart of the Buddha's message is the claim that the way to dispel my anguish and confusion is to abandon my sense of the 'self' as a fixed and solid thing. Liberation comes when I understand the self to be 'empty', a construct and a 'useful fiction'. Liberation comes when I learn to avoid the 'fallacy of misplaced concreteness' about the self.

For Buddha, and later for Nagarjuna, emptiness-of-self is a code for freedom and authenticity. Our anguish and confusion stems from our holding on to our sense of self as something to be defended and to be asserted at all costs. If I am 'empty' of this sense of 'self', I am free to live authentically – less at loggerheads with myself, more at ease in the world. As Batchelor puts it, emptiness is experienced as letting go of fixed ideas about oneself and the world. It's 'not a *state* but a *way*'. To be empty of self is no longer to be self-centred or full of oneself.

Here is how Nagarjuna put it in his writing on Self:

> Were mind and matter me,
> I would come and go like them.
> If I were something else,
> They would say nothing about me.
> Buddha said: 'it is real',

And 'it is unreal,'
And 'it is both real and unreal',
And 'it is neither one nor the other.'

In short, the self does not exist as an isolated, defined and permanent object. The more you search for it through meditation, philosophical inquiry, psychological analysis, or investigation of the brain, you will not unearth any 'thing' that corresponds to self. This is not to deny that a self exists. The self is a construct not an illusion. It exists, but not in the way we instinctively feel it does.

As I understand it, a person empty of self in this sense is a changing, evolving, functional, moral self. This echoes what modern neuroscience and cognitive science are saying about what we call the self. There appears to be a growing consensus between virtually all the reflective traditions in human history – philosophy, science, psychology and Asian meditation practices – that challenges the naïve sense of the self.

When cognitive scientists and philosophers talk about the self today they mean an 'embodied' and 'socially embedded' subject of experience, says Evan Thompson. 'Although this kind of self is a construction, it is not an illusion'.

Paradoxically, judging from the shelves of self-help literature in our bookstores, many people suffer from a poor self-image and low self-esteem rather than from an inflated sense of the self. Our modern sense of self would appear to be precarious. The Dalai Lama had great difficulty with the idea of a low self-esteem when he met with Western scientists because there is no equivalent in Tibetan thought or language.

Siddhartha Gautama did not dismiss the self as a fiction or promote a 'religion of withdrawal from the world' as is often dismissively claimed by Western writers. He likened the self to a field that needs to be irrigated and cared for so that the plants flourish. He likened himself to a doctor offering a course of treatment to heal our ills, rather than a set of dogmas that will bring us to the Truth. It's not easy to shake off the leftovers of the idea of original sin. Having been brought up on a diet containing such dark and damning purgatives as the Fall and original sin, imagine my surprise when I came across the Buddhist idea that we are all born sane. We should embrace the 'sanity we are born with', says Chogyam Trungpa. What a revolutionary idea. It has its roots in the seminal teaching of Siddhartha Gautama.

He struck out in a radical new direction. Understand the source of your suffering and accept that you are a contingent, fully formed and sane human being. This was a profoundly illuminating discovery for me. Like most people, says Batchelor, we rebel against the contingency of our existence. We recoil at having been born and having to die and fill the intervening years with all manner of things to deflect our contingency. We seem trapped into an endless cycle of wanting what we don't have, or having what we don't want. We crave to be loved and recognised and we dread rejection, failure, cancer, senility.

Our salvation, said Siddhartha Gautama, lies not in accepting some or other transcendent saviour who will rescue us from our contingency. Rather it lies in understanding the self as a project to be realised, a field of potentially fertile ground that, if carefully tended, will enable plants to flourish. He compared the self to a block of wood that can be shaped and fashioned into something of value.

I can identify with this woodwork metaphor. Nothing gives me greater pleasure than to take a rough piece of wood and turn it into a bowl on my lathe. When I took leave of the University of Venda, I needed a complete change. I'd been to the wood-turners' club exhibition at Kirstenbosch and loved what I saw. Jenny picked up the cues. Next thing, I was the proud owner of a lathe. I took a masterclass with Izak Cronje and started turning. Over the years I've turned gifts for my friends and family. Jewellery boxes, wine bottle coasters, ornaments. All in exotic woods, my favourite being wild

127

olive. There's solace to be found in my workshop when I'm crafting something from a rough piece of wood. All-absorbing, creative, an exploration of the beauty inherent in a piece of wood. A practical form of meditative thinking.

Siddhartha Gautama described himself as a doctor offering a course of therapy to bring about healing. He called this sculpting or therapy 'The Eightfold Path'. It's the cultivation of appropriate vision, thought, speech, action, livelihood, effort, mindfulness and concentration. As Batchelor puts it, he presented the path as 'a middle way that avoids the dead ends of infatuation and mortification ... indulging my appetites or punishing myself for my excesses'.

The thinker whose work had been fundamental for my journey of discovery walked to his meditation cushion, swivelled on one leg and sat in a half-lotus position, looking comfortable, serene: Stephen Batchelor. His wife, Martine, sitting upright on a chair because of a back problem, led us in a thirty-minute meditation, focusing on the breath.

I had been looking forward to this 2013 New Year event at the Emoyeni Retreat Centre in the majestic Magaliesberg. Stephen led the retreat on secular Buddhism; Martine led our meditation practice. When I was working on my PhD at UCT in 1972, Stephen, an eighteen-year-old hippie, was travelling overland from the UK to India, to Dharamasala, the capital-in-exile of the Dalai Lama. Two years later he was ordained as a novice Buddhist monk. Stephen left Tibetan Buddhism in 1981 to train in Zen Buddhism in South Korea. He disrobed in 1985 and married Martine Fages, who had been a Zen Buddhist nun in Korea for ten years.

Stephen and Martine went to England to the Sharpham Buddhist community, in Devon, where Stephen co-founded the Sharpham College for Buddhist Studies. In 2000, they moved to Aquitaine, France, where they live in a small village near Bordeaux. From this base, they both write and teach around the world.

My introduction to Stephen's writing was his *Faith to Doubt: Glimpses of Buddhist Uncertainty* (1990). At the time of the Emoyeni retreat, I had read his most recent book *Confessions of a Buddhist Atheist* (2010). These are his autobiographical books, in which he reflects on his journey from what he describes as the hermetically sealed Buddhism of Tibet through what he thought was the surprisingly closed system of Korean Zen. All the time questioning, allowing his doubts to prompt his searching. I felt I'd found a soulmate who, in another faith-tradition, was living with questions.

How was Stephen going to approach the theme of secular Buddhism at this retreat? Here was a man, fluent in English, French and German, as well as being a master of the ancient Pali texts, searching for the original genius of the Buddha by robustly interrogating both the texts and contemporary experience.

As the retreat unfolded, we were treated to an exegesis of the Pali texts in which the Buddha teaches what have come to be called the Four Noble Truths. Stephen had the entire Pali canon on his iPad and would scroll through it to find the verses that supported his argument.

And what was his argument? 'What was original about Buddha's teaching?' asked Stephen. How did he differ from the many teachers in India in his day? 'Talking about the Siddhartha Gautama's Four Noble Truths makes them sound like metaphysical claims. Claims that can be dismissed because they are not verifiable. But the Buddha made it clear that he was not interested in *the* Truth, in dogmatism, nor was he interested in metaphysical questions. He was much more pragmatic. He asked his followers to try out what he had found to be true for himself, to see if it works.'

Stephen suggested one way into this question: 'What happens if I reframe the Four Noble Truths as the Four *Tasks*?' The four tasks were illustrated by the Buddhist teacher Nanavira Thera from the story of Alice in Wonderland finding a bottle with mysterious content. The bottle's label didn't say what it contained, only what Alice was supposed to do with it: 'Drink me.' In the same way, said Nanavira, we are to treat the Four Noble Truths not as truths to be believed, but as tasks. The label on the first Buddhist bottle says 'know me' – embrace suffering where you find it, instead of avoiding it. The second says 'give me up' – let go of your craving, your grasping after what you don't have. The third says 'realise me' – experience living without craving. And the fourth urges 'develop me' – cultivate the things that will you to live with equanimity and compassion. Cultivate the practice of mindfulness.

A secular Buddhism for Stephen Batchelor takes up these four tasks – not as safe or timeless truths – but as duties undertaken for the sake of the world. What draws us to Buddhism, says Batchelor, is that 'it offers a methodology which might actually work in addressing the question of suffering'.

For some Buddhists, Batchelor is a reformer, for others he is the latest in a long line of heretics who threaten the tradition. And I knew of course that it was simply not possible to reach back into the actual teachings of Siddhartha Gautama, any more than it was with the teachings of Jesus.

I came away from the retreat thinking that here is a reformer who is uniquely placed to make Buddhism relevant to the secular modern world. But let Batchelor speak for himself: 'I (seek) to lead a life that embodies Buddhist values within the context of secularism and modernity. I have no interest in preserving the dogmas and institutions of traditional Asian forms of Buddhism as though they possessed an intrinsic value independent of the conditions under which they arose. For me Buddhism is like a living organism'.

But how does Buddhism engage with the modern world with all its ills?

'The mercy of the West has been social revolution; the mercy of the East has been individual insight into the basic self/void. We need both', says Gary Schneider. When I first discovered Buddhist meditation practice and began to read widely in Asian religion and thought, I was troubled by the question: can we deduce or derive courses of social action from Buddhism?

My doctoral dissertation had been about this question. Given the possibilities and problems of our times, what criteria do we have for deciding what to do? Niebuhr stood in what might be called the 'prophetic tradition' of the Old Testament. It is in the interplay between presuppositions held by faith (such as 'God is at work in history') and contemporary events that prophets like Amos, Isaiah or Jeremiah deduced courses of social action for their times. Niebuhr's many books reveal how he tried to derive courses of social action from the interplay between tradition (Protestant Christianity) and experience (how is the United States to conduct itself as a new superpower?).

His first venture in political philosophy was called *Moral Man and Immoral Society* (1932). 'My thesis', recalled Niebuhr many years later, is 'that collective self-regard of class, race and nation is more stubborn and persistent than the egoism of individuals'. At the time the book was considered so controversial that no British edition was published until 1966. Niebuhr's thesis is critical if we want to engage in social ethics.

And his argument, made before the Holocaust and Hiroshima, was refreshingly new: individuals behave immorally, but the wrongs perpetrated by societies or collectives are graver and more far-reaching. Also, individuals are more open to moral exhortation than societies are. Niebuhr was challenging the naive liberal utopianism he detected in America of his time.

In a career that spanned Ford's mass production of the motor car in Detroit in the 1920s to the assumption by the United States of the mantle of a superpower, Niebuhr attempted to deduce criteria for social ethics from his faith. And in the late 1960s, at the end of an illustrious career, he expressed frustration that people in positions of responsibility found they could agree with his conclusions but could not accept the presuppositions of faith from which he derived his social ethics.

Is a *Buddhist* social ethic possible? The Zen Buddhist David Loy attempted a Buddhist social theory with the publication of his *The Great Awakening: A Buddhist Social Theory* (2003). He argues that the main sources of unwholesome behaviour according to Buddhism – the roots of evil – are greed, ill-will and delusion. To end our suffering as human beings, they need to be transformed into their counterparts – greed into generosity, ill-will into loving kindness, and delusion into wisdom.

When it comes to the ills of society, Loy argues that institutionalised greed is at the root of problems such as poverty; institutionalised ill-will is at the root of war and conflict; and institutionalised delusion is the root cause of our ecological crisis. In other words, the social roots of suffering lie in our deluded sense of collective self – race, class, gender, nation or any combination of these. So far, so good. But Loy is more sanguine when it comes to poverty, war or the ecological crisis – to name just three of the challenges of our day.

He appears to end up saying something similar to what Reinhold Niebuhr said from a different standpoint and in different times, namely, that it is extremely difficult to derive criteria for social ethics from the presuppositions held by faith – whether you are a Protestant Christian or a Zen Buddhist.

I think Hans Jonas understood better than most why this is so difficult. After years of grappling with questions of social ethics, he reluctantly concluded that the reach of the challenges of the contemporary world far outstrip the ability of traditional ethical systems to deal with them. Ethical systems generated by traditional religious beliefs are inadequate for the challenges of our times. So, Jonas would say that you cannot deduce criteria for social choice from the faith-traditions of our fathers. Ours is a post-Enlightenment, disenchanted, secular, post-modern world. As I tried to show in my chapter on crafting a modern moral GPS, you have to start afresh.

Secular mindfulness practice

*I don't know about you, but my mind has
a mind of its own.*
– Guy Claxton

I'm an incorrigible browser. The first thing I look for in a new
city is a good bookshop. So, in the mid-90s, I was browsing in
the philosophy section of a bookshop on Fifth Avenue, New York,
when I came across a book called *Wherever You Go There You Are*
(1994). Apart from this intriguing title, what captured my interest
was the author. Jon Kabat-Zinn is the founder director of the Stress
Reduction Clinic at the University of Massachusetts Medical Centre
in the Division of Preventive and Behavioural Medicine. The Clinic,
founded in 1979, took the novel approach of using mindfulness
meditation derived from Buddhism in an entirely secular setting for
patients who suffered from chronic pain and stress-related disorders.

I bought the book, read it in one sitting and ordered the
guided meditation tapes by Kabat-Zinn and have been meditating
ever since.

The book could not have come at a better time for me. I had
retired early as Vice Chancellor of the University of Natal and
had just started a temporary job with the Cape Higher Education
Consortium. I was working with a Jungian analyst, trying to make
sense of this traumatic and tumultuous period in my life. And in my
mid-50s, I was naturally asking: What am I going to do with the rest
of my life?

The Tibetan word for meditation is *gom* which, roughly translated,
means 'to become familiar with'. As I learned to practice mindfulness
meditation I realised that there was much about the new 'me' of the
mid-90s that I needed to get to know. Without a real job and without
the prospects of one. No longer part of the Methodist family, and
gradually coming to the realisation that I could no longer assent

to the beliefs and practices of the Christian faith. I was in a new and unfamiliar space. 'Guess what?' writes Jon Kabat-Zinn. 'When it comes right down to it, wherever you go, there you are. Whatever you wind up doing, that's what you wound up doing. Whatever you are thinking right now, *that's* what's on your mind. Whatever has happened to you, it has already happened. The important question is, how are you going to handle it? In other words, Now what?'

Too true. This was the moment in my life that I had to work with. And Kabat-Zinn introduced me to a way of working with the moment called 'mindfulness meditation'. He explained that it was an ancient Buddhist practice that had profound relevance for today. And you don't have to become a Buddhist to practice a way of waking up and living in harmony with yourself in the world.

Music to my ears. A secular practice to train my mind which did not involve me in exchanging the baggage of Christianity for that of Buddhism! A sort of secular 'spiritual exercise', as I thought of it, which had nothing to do with God or the tenets of any religious tradition. Moreover, a practice which had much in common with developments in brain science. But I'm getting ahead of myself. Let me step back and explore just why mindfulness meditation has had such purchase in the Western world.

Remember that wonderful line in one of James Joyce's short stories: 'Mr Duffy lived a short distance from his body.' He stands for all of us who tend to live in our heads, who often find ourselves 'on autopilot', not really attending to the present moment. Those of us whose minds wander off when we're trying to concentrate and refuse to stop churning when we're trying to sleep. Those of us who seem to spend much of our time lost in past memories or anticipating a future that is not yet. 'I don't know about you', says polymath Guy Claxton, 'but my mind has a mind of its own'! I knew the feeling.

And, of course, with the advent of the computer, the Internet and the smartphone our levels of distraction are growing exponentially.

A recent article by Barclays Bank in the magazine *Intelligence* features the work of Matthew Crawford who says that distraction is a kind of 'obesity of the mind'. His larger point being that attention is the engine of the modern economy, yet it is being depleted by information technology. Attention is a finite resource that is being whittled away by distraction.

There is a growing body of research on the effects of distraction. The article quotes a startling claim that the average office worker checks their email thirty times per hour and the average smartphone user checks their phone over two hundred times per day! Even allowing for some overstating of the case, it seems that attention deficit is growing.

Picture this. A group of twenty-five people has just arrived for the first session of their eight-week Mindfulness-based Stress Reduction (MBSR) course. They are all patients at the Massachusetts Medical Centre who have voluntarily signed up for the course. Having introduced themselves and spoken about their experiences of chronic pain, anxiety or depression, they engage in the first exercise of the evening. Each one of them is closely examining a raisin. They are encouraged to bring ever more attention to its surface structure, the way it captures the light, its textures and – finally – the way it bursts its skin and meets the flood of saliva produced in its anticipation. They are eating their raisins mindfully; an exercise that can take up to ten minutes.

Kabat-Zinn defines mindfulness as 'the awareness that arises by paying attention on purpose, in the present moment, and non-judgementally'. In 1979, he discovered that mindfulness meditation helps people with difficult conditions like chronic pain, AIDS and cancer. It's not a magical 'cure' but it helps patients to relate to their stress and suffering in a different way. This course, and ones modelled on it, is used around the world today. Not only for people with illness, but for thousands of participants simply wanting to find a way to deal with normal daily difficulties of life – what Kabat-Zinn calls 'full catastrophe living'.

Typically a group meets once a week for eight weeks. The course is well defined and participatory. It teaches people to translate the same quality of attention they gave to the raisin to other aspects of their moment-by-moment experience, using guided meditation as the vehicle. Sitting meditation, walking meditation, movement exercises based on hatha yoga, body scans, poetry readings and the like. The group is given guidance to practice at home. You could say that the course is aimed at helping people to cope with stress differently. Stress is a natural response of our bodies to threat. What meditation does is to improve the person's ability to deal with their pain or anxiety or depression. Kabat-Zinn points out that the Pali word for 'suffering' can be translated as 'stress'.

In a session with the Dalai Lama, Kabat-Zinn recently explained his approach like this: 'At the heart of MBSR is an experiment to see whether we could take the essence of Buddhist meditation practise, insofar as we understand it, and somehow make it accessible to people who would not find it through a traditional Buddhist or spiritual path, but are nevertheless plagued by suffering…' In effect, Kabat-Zinn has taken the 2 500 year old Asian tradition of meditation and translated it into a secular Western setting. But the story doesn't end there.

Depression: in the 1990s, three clinical psychologists – Mark Williams, John Teasdale and Zindel Segal – were developing a new treatment for people with recurrent depression, using Cognitive Behavioural Therapy (CBT). They were inspired by Kabat-Zinn to include mindfulness in their programme. In time, the course they designed was called Mindfulness-Based Cognitive Therapy (MBCT). It has tested very favourably in trials with other approaches and is now endorsed in the UK by the National Institute for Health and Clinical Excellence for use with people who have suffered more than two episodes of depression.

A Reuters report in the *Cape Times* of 3 May 2016 tells of research that analysed data on 1258 participants from randomised trials that compared mindfulness-based cognitive therapy with other treatments for recurring depression among people who were fully or partially in remission. Overall, the MBCT group were 31% less likely to have depression again after sixty weeks compared with others who received different treatments.

Chronic pain: Vidyamala Burch founded Breathworks, in Manchester, UK, in 2004. It is based on her personal experience of using mindfulness for over twenty years to successfully manage very severe spinal pain following two major episodes of surgery and a car accident. Breathworks draws on the work of Kabat-Zinn. According to Breathworks's approach to mindfulness, human beings have the capacity for 'self-reflexive consciousness, i.e. an ability to be objective about subjective mental, emotional and physical experiences'. It makes the point that people who are living with pain, illness or stress tend to be dominated by their suffering. They tend to become trapped in aversive or avoidant states, thus becoming victims. Mindfulness teaches us how to investigate present-moment experience with awareness. It helps the person distinguish between 'primary suffering' – the stressor, such as spinal injury, and 'secondary suffering' – the ways in which the sufferer *reacts* to the primary suffering.

Breathworks offers an array of online and residential courses. It's well worth visiting its website at breathworks-mindfulness.org.uk.

Jon Kabat-Zinn completed his PhD in molecular biology. His thesis supervisor was Salvador Luria, who shared the Nobel Prize in medicine and physiology in 1969 with physicist Max Delbruck. In 2011, Kabat-Zinn took stock of the scientific evidence for the benefits of mindfulness. He says, 'the scientific investigation of mindfulness and its effects on health and well-being has grown tremendously over this (25 year) period.' In 2005, more than a hundred papers were published on mindfulness and its clinical applications; in 2013, there were more than one and a half thousand, plus an ever-increasing number of books on the subject. There are still methodological problems to be ironed out, but the rigour of research in this area is steadily improving.

Part of the reason for this growing body of literature is the explosion in brain research and neuroscience. When I was at school, we were taught that the size and circuitry of the brain are fixed before adulthood. But in the last fifteen years or so, neuroscientists and psychologists have demonstrated that the adult brain is capable of neuroplasticity – forming new cells and pathways. As Sharon Salzberg says, 'The brain rewires and reshapes itself in response to environment, experience, and training. And meditation is one of those brain-changing experiences. A number of recent studies confirm that meditation can bring about significant physiological changes in the brain that create welcome changes in health, mood, and behaviour.'

Picture this. We're in a quiet room in the neurology ward of the Waisman Laboratory for Brain Imaging at the University of Wisconsin. A shaven-headed Tibetan monk lies down on a sterile trolley and is inserted into a functional MRI scanner – a large tubular magnet that allows electrical impulses and radio waves to be converted into images of the brain. The monk settles his concentration, steadies his body and, having achieved a state of awareness, cultivates compassion. He presses a button each time he reaches and stabilises a mental state. On the other side of the chamber young neuroscientists register the real time activities of his brain. Daniel Goleman summarises the results of this ground-breaking research on a handful of meditation adepts. 'During meditation on compassion, neural activity in a key centre in the brain's system for happiness jumped by 700 to 800 percent! For ordinary subjects in the study, volunteers who had just begun to meditate, that same area increased its activity by … 10 to 15 per cent'.

Google it or cast your eye along the shelves of local bookshops and you'll see how the popularity of mindfulness has surged over the past few years. There seems to be a mindfulness book for every conceivable malady. There are even apps you can download on your cellphone. The *Headspace* app offers ten-minute guided meditations and has millions of users worldwide. The company is worth a fortune.

Large companies and organisations like Google, Apple, Sony, Ikea and the London Department of Health and Transport have adopted mindfulness meditation as part of their employee packages. They claim that it increases productivity and reduces sick leave. It is available as a treatment on the NHS in the UK. There's an active Mindfulness Institute in South Africa, and you can get training in mindfulness at the University of Stellenbosch. Some South African business schools are including modules on mindfulness in their courses.

You can see why some critics are calling it a 'tool' of capitalism, designed to keep the workforce attentive and focussed. Slavoj Zizek has even called it, echoing Marx, the new 'opiate of the people'. Ronald Purser has written a whole book on this subject, called *McMindfulness: How Mindfulness Meditation became the New Capitalist Spirituality* (2019). The essence of this type of critique is that, of course, large corporations are interested in anything that promises to improve the wellbeing of their employees and which makes them more productive!

Critics like Evan Thompson offer a different assessment. He is a student of Asian traditions, has practiced mindfulness and is thoroughly familiar with neuroscientific research into meditation. His point is that the modern Western adaptation of mindfulness meditation is guilty of two errors. First, it separates meditation from its ethical roots in the Buddha's teaching. Second, he questions its facile practice of claiming support from neuroscience. 'People are mindful, not brains', he says. Much of the hype about mindfulness meditation seems to disembody us. Phrases like 'headspace' and 'mindful brain' seem to be saying we are our brains. It is bad neuroscience. Cognitive science speaks of the embodied being embedded in society, history and culture. Thompson draws the following conclusion from his critique: 'The idea that mindfulness is in the head feeds the current mindfulness mania. It reinforces selfish individualism … (even) consumerism by making mindfulness into a commodity that an individual can try to acquire.'

It must be said that practicing mindfulness is a brave thing to do. It means that you are willing to be alone with yourself – to be present to your own body and mind. And that's the time when the things you have buried come bubbling to the surface. So, it's not surprising that experienced mindfulness meditators and teachers caution that mindfulness meditation is not for everyone. It's not a quick fix or panacea. It's not an easy way to de-stress!

The research on mindfulness practice has largely ignored the negative side-effects of mindfulness. One qualitative study showed that its application is not ideal for everyone. There are texts that are hundreds of years old that do touch on the negative side of contemplation – sometimes called 'the dark night of the soul'.

This is why Ken Wilber, for one, stresses that people should not practice mindfulness meditation if they actually need psychotherapy. Where there is light, there is shadow. The dark side of the psyche – those aspects of the self that we split off, reject, deny and repress – are likely to bubble up when we meditate. And that can be unnerving if you do not have an experienced teacher or counsellor to turn to. Mindfulness is not to be confused with psychotherapy. This is why in the UK there are now guidelines for teachers of mindfulness to try to ensure credible course offerings.

The famous naturalist, E. O. Wilson, used the unusual word 'consil-ience' to describe those breakthrough moments when knowledge from different aspects of human experience literally 'jumps together' to create a common groundwork from which we can move forward. I think we may be on the threshold of such a moment. The ongoing conversation between practioners of contemplative traditions, East and West, and the sciences of the brain may well lead to a new consilience.

Only when I started meditating did I realise that my mind seems to have a mind of its own. It wanders off when I'm trying to concentrate. It chatters away incessantly, flitting from one thing to another – can I say 'mindlessly'? It refuses to stop churning over the day when I try to sleep. One way to understand Buddhist mindfulness meditation is to think of it as training the mind – something Buddhists have been doing for two and a half millennia.

Meditation, I have discovered, is the simple exercise of resting in the natural state of your present mind, allowing yourself to be present to whatever thoughts, feelings, sensations or emotions occur. Using the breath as an anchor, you get in touch with yourself and experience a sense of calm and peace. In this state of expanded openness, or mindfulness, you begin to gain insight, you see things as they are and accept them for what they are. This form of meditation is called 'insight meditation'.

This is liberating. Instead of your untamed and untrained chattering-monkey-mind carrying on and on, you become aware of your thoughts, feelings, sensations or emotions as they arise. As one teacher whose name I cannot recall put it: 'Let it come. Let it be. Let it go'. In other words, don't fight your thoughts, don't engage them, don't push them away and don't cling to them in morbid introspection. Let them arise, let them be whatever they are and let them go in their own time. Whether it is something beautiful or something ugly, just stay with the breath calmly in that moment.

Sound simple and easy? It's neither simple nor easy. I suppose that's why mindfulness meditation is called a 'practice', something you have to do on a regular basis if you want to become skilful. Being in the present moment, really present, is a novel experience for most people when they first attempt mindfulness meditation. We seem to spend our lives on autopilot. So much of our lives spent unawares – the mind chattering away. So much of our lives spent trying to avoid pain and hanging on to pleasure for all it's worth, pushing away what hurts and clinging to what is comfortable and pleasant. Being present in the moment is startling, even unsettling.

I wish I could remember which Tibetan teacher said this, but the quote stayed with me: 'When the mind is not altered, it is clear. When water is undisturbed, it is transparent.' Whatever comes up, just be present to it. That's the essence. There are no good thoughts, and no bad thoughts. There are just thoughts that come and go. There are no good feelings and bad feelings. There are just feelings that come and go. A Tibetan adept might say he is really 'a process of non-judgmental awareness. When we meditate we adopt the objective perspective of a scientist toward our own subjective experience.'

Practitioners speak of this very moment as the 'perfect teacher' – and it is 'always with us'. They make the point that we tend to regard discomfort in any form as bad news. Mindfulness meditation enables me to open up rather than shut down. It's an invitation to notice when I have reached my limit and not to get carried away by hope or fear, but rather attend to these emotions. By being with what is going on, and not dissociating from it, I gain awareness, I come alive.

In this space, I am not caught up in my own version of reality, my stories. This is where we start with accepting ourselves, warts and all. By training the mind not to fixate on the good or the bad, I learn to have compassion. And, to the degree that I have compassion for myself, I feel compassion for others. Compassion is part of the practice; we can learn it.

The practice of compassion (*tonglen*) takes in pain with the conscious in-breath and sends out wellbeing with the out-breath. It turns our normal way of reacting on its head. Instead of pushing pain and suffering away and grasping for wellbeing, the practice is to breathe in the pain and suffering 'with the wish that everyone could be free of pain'. Whenever we encounter happiness in any form, the instruction is to breathe it out – send it out, so everyone can feel joy. The practice of compassion, says Pema Chödrön, 'reverses the usual logic of avoiding suffering and seeking pleasure'. We become liberated from our patterns of selfishness. We begin to feel love for both ourselves and others, awakened to a bigger reality.

This practice of compassion is sometimes called 'loving kindness meditation'. It requires awareness of breath and imagination. It recognises that just as I want to achieve happiness and avoid suffering, others feel the same way. I bring this realisation to my practice. I name those I know to be suffering. And, in my imagination I reach out to all sufferers I don't know. It challenges us to live mindfully so that our unborn neighbours of tomorrow can inherit a world fit to live in.

One form of Zen meditation involves the conscious and disciplined use of *questioning*. Again it sounds easy but it's not. A traditional *koan* question is 'What is this?' There is no English word for *koan*. It's a story or puzzle that invokes further questions and that cannot be answered by intellectual inquiry. There are nearly two thousand official Zen *koan*s, past stories aimed at realising enlightenment through a process of questioning, such as: 'What is the sound of one hand clapping?' *Koan*s also help you to see life as funny rather than tragic. Here is an example: 'Where do we go when we die?' asked the student. 'I shall go straight to hell,' said the old master. 'You,' said the questioner, 'a good Zen master?' 'If I don't, who will teach you?'

In meditation practice, the Zen *koan* 'What is this?' is intended to open the practitioner up – a bit like diving off a board into a pool of questioning. I am not asking, 'What is this thought?', for example. Rather, I am asking, 'What is it that is thinking?' or 'Before you think, what is this?'

As Martine and Stephen Batchelor explain in *What Is This? An-*

cient Questions for Modern Minds (2019), the practice calls for going behind my veil of certainty, my sense of myself, to that place where questions are allowed to arise. And to live with the questions, to experience uncertainty, even bewilderment, to get me out of my comfort zone. It is to cultivate 'great doubt' by short-circuiting the brain's 'answer-giving habit' (my normal I-have-an-answer-for-every-question response). That's a habit I surely need to break. Asking the question 'What is this?' is the sort of earthy, primary questioning and wondering that gives rise to philosophy and religion – it's about the mystery and meaning of it all.

This form of questioning has been called 'quiet focused astonishment'. Awe, perhaps? Waiting in pregnant silence, before thinking and thoughts? It is to value unknowing; not to be afraid to ask questions and confront your finite-ness, your mortality, your fallibility – to let go of the 'consolation of certainty'.

It is liberating to apply meditation practice to life, to lean into the overwhelming sense of failure, disappointment, despair or sadness that sometimes comes our way, and to consciously, mindfully live with it. We befriend the emotional state instead of trying to eradicate it.

You could say that mindfulness meditation is a form of therapy for the sane. Sharon Salzberg, a founder of the Insight Meditation Society in America, has been practising and teaching for some thirty years. I can attest to the benefits of meditation she has identified:

◇ You'll begin to spot the unexamined assumptions that get in the way of happiness.
◇ You'll stop limiting yourself.
◇ You'll weather hard times better.
◇ You'll rediscover a deeper sense of what's really important to you.
◇ You'll have a portable emergency resource.

◇ You'll be in closer touch with the best parts of yourself.

◇ You'll recapture the energy you've been wasting trying to control the uncontrollable.

◇ You'll understand how to relate to change better – to accept that it's inevitable and believe that it's possible.

In a fairly recent book aimed at the general public, *Mindfulness: A Practical Guide to Finding Peace in a Frantic World* (2011), Mark Williams and Danny Penman say, 'For many years it was assumed that we all have an emotional thermostat which determines how happy we are in life'. Some people were thought to have a happy disposition, others not. This emotional set-point was presumed to be encoded in our genes'. All this was shattered when Richard Davidson and Jon Kabat-Zinn discovered that 'mindfulness training allowed people to escape the gravitational pull of their emotional set-point'. Further research shows that for people who meditate over several years the emotional thermostat can be *reset*, for the better.

How does this work? Through mindfulness meditation you become aware of your emotions and bodily sensations as they arise. And you learn to deal with them more skilfully. We all make the mistake of thinking that emotions are problems to be solved through rational critical thinking. I know I do. Unhappiness, fear, despair, stress or anxiety cannot be solved; they can only be *felt*. If I allow myself to become aware of what I feel, the feeling is much more likely to disappear naturally. Buddhist meditation masters have been taught this skilful awareness for millennia. Mindfulness-based cognitive therapy research and practice corroborates this. As Williams and Penman observe, 'If you stop and reflect for a moment, the mind doesn't just think. It can also be *aware* that it is thinking. It's like … a vantage point – from which you can see everything for miles around … It allows you to step outside the chattering negative self-talk and your reactive impulses and emotions.'

145

My mindfulness meditation

I prefer to practise early in the morning, before the day begins. In a corner in my study, I place a stool (I can't sit in a lotus position because of a bad knee). This particular morning, I've set my timer for twenty minutes. I strike my Tibetan begging bowl gently; I bought it at the Tibetan Teahouse in Simon's Town, of all places, yet paradoxically the location of my first parish. I listen to the resonance of the brass as I prepare to sit, back straight, eyes closed and hands touching on my lap. It's quiet, the air is still, and in the distance I can hear a dog barking. I rock gently backwards, forwards and sideways so I am relaxed but firm in posture.

I begin to count to ten on the out-breath. Breathing from my abdomen, my mind begins to focus but I lose count. Following your breath sounds easy but it's hard to do. I begin to count again. I say the words, 'May the actions I take towards the good, towards understanding myself, towards being mindful and at ease, be of benefit to others today.' I try to say them following my breath.

Now I sit, breathing in and breathing out, pausing at each out-breath before breathing in again. Thoughts come, and thoughts go. I let them come, I let them stay as long as they will, and I let them go. I imagine myself a riverbed over which good and bad thoughts and experiences flow. I do not become entangled with them. They are indicators not directors of my life. I try not to cling to bad feelings and experiences in morbid introspection. I let go even of the good. 'When the butterfly settles in your hand, do not close it.'

At some point I think compassionately of a close friend whose husband died recently, of two friends who are suffering from the same degenerative disease, of someone whose marriage is breaking up. I hold them in mind, saying, 'May you be free from harm of any kind, may you experience a sense of wellbeing even in your suffering, may you live with ease today.'

I am surprised to hear the timer, signalling the end of the session. I strike my begging bowl and rise to its receding sounds.

146

Living without gods

The role of a writer is not to say what we can all say,
but what we are unable to say.
– Anaïs Nin

That night in Kalk Bay when, in my teens, I experienced connectedness with all things, I interpreted it within the framework of Protestant Christianity. Years later, I discovered a passage in a book by the great theologian Paul Tillich that spoke to the same experience:

> Sometimes at that moment a wave of light breaks into our darkness, and it is as though a voice were saying, 'You are accepted. *You are accepted*, accepted by that which is greater than you, and the name of which you do not know. Do not ask for the name now; perhaps you will find it later. Do not try to do anything; perhaps later you will do much. Do not seek for anything; do not perform anything; do not intend anything. *Simply accept the fact that you are accepted.*' If that happens to us, we experience grace.

I now know that my Kalk Bay experience was mystical. Psychologist Guy Claxton says that common to these experiences is a sense of aliveness, of mystery, of feeling at home and of being at peace with the world. I can attest to that.

I have since had other mystical experiences, what I call 'signals of transcendence'. Listening to Handel's music, walking in the gardens at Kirstenbosch, watching the sun set over the sea at Scarborough, making love, or standing before the Pyramids in Egypt. In such moments I experience the world with wonder and awe.

Sadly, there are also those moments when what we see is so conflicting, so jarring, that we are aghast and appalled. I think of

Kevin Carter's famous photograph of a Sudanese child, a mere skeleton, watched closely by a vulture. An image so discordant that my sense of offence was overwhelming. Carter, who won international acclaim for the photo, later committed suicide.

Is it possible to experience a sense of transcendence if you do not believe in God? This and other questions have pursued me throughout the years when I was a practising Christian, years when I no longer had any real sense of faith in God, years when I was crafting a secular spirituality.

When I originally wrote about my Kalk Bay experience, my friend Randall Falkenberg, whom I had known since our time at Rhodes University, commented: 'Your view of transcendence seems to me to be far more mystical and Buddhist than my own. Nothing wrong with that, of course! In fact, it raises the possibility of a dialogue of differences in our joint work together.'

'My hard-headed atheism,' Randall continued, 'would say of course you are a "child of the universe" and of course the universe is both greater than you and you are a part of it – that is what the concept "universe" means. So, for me this affirmation is not an act of faith, not even "secular faith". It is simply a statement of fact without any religious or spiritual overlay or interpretation. Also, Tillich makes such a big deal of the experience of "a wave of light that breaks into our darkness" and a seeming voice that says "You are accepted …" etc. That's fine for poetic or dramatic writing and thinking and it may address feelings that some people may experience; its wonderful oratory but it is prior to the "total absence of God" that I (and many others) experience.' What is the 'total absence of God'? Can you experience transcendence when God is absent? Is mysticism only possible when God is 'present'? Is 'secular spirituality' not a contradiction in terms? In opening to these questions, I found André Comte-Sponville's argument for spirituality without God helpful. Man is a spiritual being, he asserts. It is not necessary to amputate that part of his humanity which we call the spiritual because he no longer believes in God. Comte-Sponville makes the case for seeing spirituality as a 'function' rather than some divine thing that exists somewhere in our bodies. Spirit is a function, a capacity, the ability to act. Spirit is that part of us which is able to think, to will, to imagine, to crack jokes, to tell stories, to experience signals of transcendence.

For me, transcendence is being at one with Jung's collective two-million-year-old self that is humankind, when all that goes into making up me is grounded in this sense of continuity and connected-ness. Although I speak of transcendence, are we not getting close to what I would like to call a 'spirituality of immanence'? What is that? For the ancient Greeks and Taoists and the modern, post-Enlightenment Buddhist, there is nothing self-contradictory in the notion of spirituality without God. And they would not equate spirituality with religion, if by religion you mean belief in supernatural being(s). As Wittgenstein says, 'Not how the world is, is the mystical, but that it is.'

I am using the words 'transcendence', 'secular spirituality' and 'mysticism' interchangeably. This exercise in retrieval is not a philosophical treatise, after all. I am attempting to join the wooden pieces, to mount the lid to the box I'm turning on my lathe, to connect my experiences and my sources – the books and ideas and people – that have helped me to fashion my approach to 'living without gods'.

Some years ago, I found the following in a Jewish prayer book in a Reformed synagogue: 'I cannot be religious without belonging to a particular religion any more than I can talk without using a particular language.' Well, I'm not sure about this. If you can't be religious without belonging to a particular religion any more than you can talk without using a particular language, must you keep quiet? Be like King Lear in the storm? 'No, I will be the pattern of all patience / I will say nothing'?

Is it possible to liberate the word 'religion', to reinvent it to denote the ultimate questions about meaning that we are interested in dealing with in this book, questions that ought not to be overshadowed by God, but which remain *religious* – what other word can we use? – in their essence? The Latin verb *religare* means 'to bind or connect'.

In 1998, Jenny and I spent three and half weeks in that part of India that was settled by war – the north. Our itinerary was arranged by our Indian friend Sharda Nayak. Our guides were all graduates, who exemplified the pressures of modernity. 'In pre-modern India,' said our guide in Udaipur, 'you would not have married without the advice of an astrologer. Today it's optional; the choice is yours.' Many of our guides did not believe that your stars need to be in alignment before you married, but they admitted that they would consult an astrologer anyway. One's fate was once determined, inexorable – now it is open to choice. But there's no harm in hedging your bets, is there?

Modernisation has not led to the decline of religion; witness the resurgence of Christianity in the United States, and of Islam worldwide. But the sacred canopy is precarious. And modernity has made it so.

Rival ethical and cultural values compete for our attention and support in the marketplace called modernity. Put another way, values are relativised. Today, when confronted with competing choices, we find ourselves asking: Whose justice? Which rationality? What authority?

Take the life-and-death question of assisted suicide. When I asked my students whether they favoured euthanasia as a means of 'easeful death' (a term used by Mary Warnock and Elizabeth Macdonald in *Easeful Death: Is There a Case for Assisted Dying?*, 2008), the majority usually said no. When I asked the same students how they would react if their terminally ill mother asked for help to die, they changed their position. Easeful death is constrained by law in South Africa. But there are countries where people can choose to obtain assistance to die.

It would appear, then, that the forces of modernisation and secularisation have weakened religion as a sacred canopy. It is precariously unstable, but there is no predicting that it will disappear.

The doomsayers who herald the end of religion have got it wrong. Whether we are people of faith or secularists, today we share an immanent frame. Our world is fundamentally different from the worlds that gave birth to the great axial religions of Judaism, Christianity and Islam in the West or Hinduism and Buddhism in the East. We cannot avoid the cognitive dissonance between beliefs that originated then and today's challenges.

As David Loy puts it, neither Moses nor the Buddha 'knew anything about the cellular structure of organisms, the genetic code of life, the microbial cause of most diseases, the periodic table of atomic elements, the structure of the solar system, Newton's laws of motion, the physics of light and electromagnetism, or the theory of relativity' – or evolution, I might add. I must confess I know little about these concepts, but I know that they have fundamentally changed our way of being in the world. We live in a world in which Einstein's famous formula means that the threats of nuclear war, nuclear accidents and nuclear weapons haunt us constantly.

In this secular age we all share a way of looking at and experiencing the world. Modern Christians, Jews, Muslim, Buddhists, Hindus, secularists, atheists – we all share it. It's not that science and technology make it impossible to believe in God. Modernity forces you to choose to do so. Many people in the contemporary West, and increasingly elsewhere, are unable to profess belief in traditional religious orthodoxies, it seems. But neither are they content with the strident certainties of modern atheism. Most of us wander about in an uncomfortable, transitional terrain where there is little agreement about the way forward.

I understand what Karen Armstrong means when she uses the word 'unknowing' to describe the temper of the first half of the twentieth century in the West. Why? Because the century started with scientists and others predicting an era of unparalleled progress as science cracked the code of nature and technology was put to the service of humanity. Sadly, these predictions turned out to be wrong, and dramatically so.

The First World War saw the slaughter of a whole generation of young men. My father fought in the trenches of France. Like so many, he was gassed and suffered from chronic emphysema. I can still see him struggling for breath as he leaned into the south easterly wind while making his way to work.

The utter futility of a war fought in the trenches for no compelling ideological or humanitarian reason saw a kind of nihilism descend on Europe. What was the meaning of it all? The most advanced countries in Europe had succeeded in crippling themselves and their opponents with their new military technology. The war machine, with its latest administrative systems for everything from conscription to troop movements to the manufacture of weapons, was efficiency itself. But to what end?

After the Armistice it was but a short step from the ensuing decline in the economy to the Great Depression of the 1930s to the rise of Fascism and Communism. A mere decade later the unthinkable happened; the world became embroiled in a second global war.

Modern secular ideologies proved as lethal as those driven by religious intolerance. Steven Pinker estimates that some 120 million people died at the hands of these ideologies in the twentieth century. And in South Africa, 1948 saw the start of a piece of ideologically driven social engineering that was to cost the lives of countless souls and scar the nation, perhaps irrevocably.

Modern science was founded on the belief that it was possible to achieve objective certainty, verifiable truth. Based on this premise, scientists at the turn of the twentieth century were predicting unfettered progress. It was only in the early twentieth century that Newton's great system was superseded by the likes of Max Planck's quantum theory, Albert Einstein's theory of relativity and Werner Heisenberg's principle of indeterminacy. Yes, these were paradigm shifts. Scientific orthodoxy had assumed that knowledge would increase incrementally. But the 1920s changed all that. As Einstein himself said, 'It was as if the ground had been pulled from under me, with no firm foundation to be seen anywhere upon which one could have built.' Unknowing, says Armstrong, 'seemed to be built into the human condition.'

The shaking of Europe's foundations in the first half of the twentieth century influenced the work of Karl Popper, whom I referred to earlier – another of my intellectual heroes. His work on the poverty of historicism, and on the nature of open societies, profoundly affected my generation. What attracted me to his work was his view that human knowledge proceeds from our problems and our attempts to solve them. Science and politics are problem-solving activities.

Two things stand out about Popper's work, which was born out of the events of the war and its aftermath: his refutation of the idea of the 'inevitability of historical progress' (a claim underpinning totalitarian regimes), and his defence of 'open societies' (liberal democracy). 'Those who promise us paradise on earth never produced anything but a hell', says Popper. *The Poverty of Historicism* (1944) is an impassioned and powerful critique of all forms of totalitarianism. The book has the following dedication: 'In memory of the countless men and women of all creeds or nations or races who fell victims to the fascist and communist belief in Inexorable Laws of Historical Destiny'.

Common to these totalising ideologies is the belief that history develops according to certain principles towards a determinate end: the socialist revolution promises a 'classless society'; the Third Reich promised a thousand years of peace: apartheid promised a 'separate but equal' future for all South Africans. All such assurances are premised on a flawed view of history.

Why should we believe the myth of revolution? Why should we

accept terror today on the promise of a humane tomorrow? What could possibly falsify such a claim? How can you know in advance that the suffering you are asking people to endure today will lead to a classless society tomorrow? 'The fundamental thesis of my book,' writes Popper, is 'that the belief in historical destiny is sheer superstition, and that there can be no prediction of the course of human history by scientific or any other rational methods.'

As far as Popper was concerned, nothing can in principle falsify the myth of revolution. Not now and not anytime in the future. The same can be said of the claims of the Third Reich and of the architects of apartheid.

We must count the costs of such claims. As Peter Berger says, the most pressing moral imperative in any policy-making is a 'calculus of pain', including who exacts it and who pays it.

Capitalism assures us that while we may experience hunger today we can expect an affluent tomorrow. How do we know? What could possibly falsify such a claim, now or anytime in the future? And who pays the price? Applying Berger's calculus: who goes hungry, jobless, homeless today awaiting the promised trickle down of capitalist bounty tomorrow?

Utopian social engineering of the communist (or apartheid) kind is fundamentally flawed. You may be able to centralise power but, in complex societies, it is impossible to centralise all the knowledge necessary for the wise wielding of that centralised power. Centralised power tends to destroy knowledge because it cannot tolerate critical thought, so the greater the centralisation of power the greater the loss of knowledge. This is one of the reasons that, in Popper's terms, these societies are closed.

Social problem-solving is complex and difficult. What we need is more problem-solving and less ideology. We need to acknowledge our inherent fallibility and be willing to learn by trial and error. In matters of science and society, it seems, we are on an unending quest for solutions to problems that will make life better for ourselves and our unborn neighbours of tomorrow. Since we cannot know in advance what will and will not work, we need *in principle* and *in practice* to remain open to possibilities, for our solutions remain fallible. There are no definite solutions.

I turn, with some trepidation, to another sense of 'unknowing', one that I've grappled with for half a lifetime. I went from the security of my faith in the Methodist God to identifying with Julian Barnes and missing God and then to a point when I realised that I didn't miss him, in the sense that I was no longer nostalgic about the comforts and consolations of religion. And I do understand the important role that the monotheistic family of religions has played in the history of the West. I am a product of that history.

I realised that I was no longer a theist, but I was not an atheist because atheism has its counterpoint in theism; it's a reactive position. At that juncture in my life, I suppose I could best describe myself as being agnostic. Agnostic, it's worth repeating, in T. H. Huxley's sense: 'In matters of the intellect, do not pretend that conclusions are certain which are not demonstrated and demonstrable.' I was certain that I was no longer certain.

It was only when I began to grapple with a tradition not premised on the existence of God, namely Buddhism, that I began to understand at an existential level what 'non-theism' might possibly mean. Even that concept, though, seems to be flawed because it also appears to be reactive to theism.

I can well remember my sense of surprise, even enlightenment, when I began to make sense of East-Asian thought. Siddhartha Gautama flew in the face of the orthodoxies of his day. In the words of Stephen Batchelor, he 'rejected the idea that freedom or salvation lay in gaining privileged access to an eternal, non-contingent source or ground, whether it be called *Atman* or God, Pure Consciousness or the Absolute'.

Here indeed was an 'immanent tradition', one which made a

great deal of sense to me intellectually and at the level of experience. Gautama valued a deep unknowing that refuses the consolations of certainty. Of course, not even the Buddha can say whether God or gods 'exist'. We don't know, and, it seems we can *never* know. We must live with the unknowing.

One of the vows recited daily in Zen Buddhist monasteries is this: 'The way is inconceivable, we vow to attain it'. It's a vow that fell strangely on my ears. Isn't religion supposed to answer questions like: Does God exist? How did the world begin? Why is there evil in the world? What happens to us when we die?

The Buddha, it seems, adopted a form of 'methodological atheism' 2 500 years ago when he refused to be drawn on whether or not God or gods exist. He bracketed metaphysical questions, saying that they are speculative and cannot be answered using our rational, problem-solving brains. Put another way, God or the gods cannot be found at the end of a reasoned argument, or at the end of a microscope or telescope, or any other extension of our senses that technology can devise.

This is not the same as the response of the Abrahamic tradition, which says that God is not and cannot be an object of thinking, an object among other objects, to be studied and reasoned about. In the Torah, the Old Testament and the Koran, God cannot be named, nor are we permitted to make any image of him – though I think Sufis may disagree with them.

156

The Buddha's position was radically different. It's not that we have failed to grasp transcendence through reason or meditation. According to Raimundo Panikkar, 'Neither cosmology nor theology, let alone anthropology encompasses the mystery of reality, according to the Buddha'. The Buddha's answer consists in giving no answer because any answer cannot avoid the trap of becoming reified, objectified and made part of a system, an '-ology' of sorts. The Buddha is *silent* about God or the gods. He makes no reply 'because he eliminates the question', says Panikkar.

As a Westerner, I found *The Silence of God* (1990) profoundly disturbing. Says Panikkar, it has been a peculiarity of Western thought from Plato onwards, 'to assume that asking ultimate questions regarding the meaning of existence is a sign of culture, of a "humane" degree of civilisation. Religion was regarded as the source of responses to such questions, so as to render one's life fully human.' No, says the Buddha. If questions of the existence of God or life after death, which are said to be of such vital importance, were actually so, they 'would not present uncertainties of any kind'. But they do. There is no end to our speculations – we all have them.

The Buddha leaves such questions out of consideration because they are 'superfluous', and because any possible response is bound to be 'vacuous'. For Panikkar they are superfluous because we can spend our lives searching for answers to questions that cannot be answered. This searching is one of the reasons we are in a constant state of malaise and discontent. And our answers are vacuous because the questions we ask, as contingent human beings, can only have answers as contingent as the questions. No 'answer to a contingent question will ever rise above contingency', so for the Buddhist 'all schools of metaphysics are peas in a pod'.

The Buddha is not an agnostic. Contingent human beings cannot leap over their own shadows, says Panikkar. The question has no satisfactory answer; if it did, we would turn contingency into an 'absolute'. Whatever else that means, it can't be a definition of God, who, on any characterisation you care to name, is not contingent.

What the Buddha would have us understand is that our questioning is based on a false presupposition, 'deriving as it does from the illusion that the creature must be able to leap over his own shadow ... the question is unintelligible in itself. One does not know what one is asking.'

The Buddha's position, says Panikkar, is 'surprisingly modern. It does not pretend that religions give us solutions. It seeks to withdraw human beings from their wish to play the little God –

to read a part not written for them.' And when you are not trying to read a part not written for you, *you* don't have answers; you accept your contingency and impermanence. And that is the 'leap of faith' the Buddha invites us to take. The 'authentic silence of the mind' which is not about speculation, even doctrine, but meditation, contemplation. 'Cultivate concentration,' says the Buddha, 'for the *bikkhu* (monk) with a concentrated mind knows things as they really are.'

In the Pali texts, the Buddha compares a man who is preoccupied with metaphysical speculations about the existence of God or life after death to a man who has been wounded by a poisoned arrow. The man refuses to have it removed until he knows who fired it; what sort of bow it was; what sort of tip the arrow had. The only concern the man should have is to get the arrow removed. The rest is beside the point.

In another well-known Pali discourse, Gautama compares people who are obsessed with answering such questions to a group of blind men who are summoned by a king to describe an elephant. Each blind person is invited to touch a different part of the animal. The one holding the trunk declares that the elephant is a tube; the one feeling the side says that the elephant is a wall; while the one holding the tail is convinced that the elephant is a rope. Preoccupation with metaphysics not only fails to deal with human suffering, but also lends itself to a restricted and distorted picture of the human situation.

I'm no expert on the Pali texts. Stephen Batchelor is. He says that Gautama's original approach was 'therapeutic and pragmatic rather than speculative and metaphysical'. My surprise, even enlightenment, with my discovery of another way in Buddhism was the realisation that having dropped one set of beliefs I didn't have to pick up another. What spoke to me in Gautama's approach was his emphasis on making *this* life – yes, experience – significant. Before taking up this theme, I want to return briefly to the issue of atheism.

Judging from our bookstores, atheism has been given fresh impetus with the strident polemical writings of the likes of Richard Dawkins, Sam Harris, Daniel Dennett and Christopher Hitchens – the 'new atheists'.

They write with the fervour of evangelical fundamentalists, preaching their message that religion is the source of all the problems of the world, the source of 'absolute evil' that poisons everything. They see themselves 'in the vanguard of a scientific/ rational movement that will eventually expunge the idea of God from human consciousness', says Karen Armstrong. Stirring stuff indeed.

What could possibly count against, falsify, their message? The atheism of Dawkins and company is parasitic upon a particular form of theism that few reflective theists would recognise. They all seem to equate religious faith with mindless naïveté. In *The God Delusion* (2006), Dawkins writes: 'I shall define the God Hypothesis ...: *there exists a superhuman, supernatural intelligence who deliberately designed and created the universe and everything in it, including us.*'

A witty and polemical response to Dawkins came from Terry Eagleton, one of Britain's foremost literary critics, who would describe himself as a Christian and a Marxist. He argues that Christian theology does not see God the Creator as 'some kind of mega-manufacturer or cosmic chief executive officer, as the Richard Dawkins school of nineteenth-century liberal rationalism tends to imagine'. Dawkins seems to think that Christianity offers a rival view of the universe to science, 'a kind of bogus theory or pseudo-explanation of the world.'

159

The debate rages on, and the criticisms mount against the new atheists. But, as many commentators have noted, like all fundamentalists, the new atheists believe they alone are in possession of the truth.

It was the advent of the new atheists that enabled me to understand better the organic link between theism, atheism and modernity.

The theism that Dawkins and company attack is itself a product of modernity. And, whatever else one might say about modernity, it moved human beings to centre stage. With the proper application of reason and the scientific method, modern men and women believed they could master and control the natural world. God, like everything else, became an *object* of thought and study.

I think Terry Eagleton is right. No committed Jew, Christian or Muslim believes in the God the new atheists attack so vigorously. The problem with the new atheists is that their science and philosophy is so much more sophisticated than their theology. They create a caricature of the God of the Abrahamic family of religions and then proceed to demolish it. For Jews, Christian and Muslims, God is not a 'hypothesis'.

In the seventeenth century, Blaise Pascal proposed a wager in his posthumously published *Pensées* (1670) – the prize being eternal life. Suppose metaphysical argument leaves us none the wiser about God's existence. Is it better to bet on God's existence? If God exists, then it is clearly better, given the prospect of eternal bliss for believers. Unbelievers, needless to say, lose out eternally. If God does not exist, then our loss is negligible. Clearly, belief is the better bet. But however you throw the dice still requires a 'leap of faith'. My non-theism, too, is a leap of faith. I rattle the dice in my hand.

Does all this mean that I am against metaphysics, that I think metaphysics unhelpful? Thinking about thinking is something we humans do. And it's called metaphysics. It was Socrates who first insisted that we must rise above whatever viewpoint we happen to hold if we are going to find a better way. Metaphysics is about using our ability to ask questions and to reflect on our answers to arrive at greater moral clarity. We cannot do without it any more than we can do without a good theory. But we don't accept metaphysical statements on face value, any more than we would accept some theory.

For much of my intellectual odyssey I was influenced by analytical philosophy, from Antony Flew to Karl Popper. *The* important questions for me were about falsification. How do we know something is true? Take a statement like 'God loves us like a father', or 'History bends towards justice'. How do we know? What would count against it? Now that I reflect on this aspect of my odyssey, I realise that the appeal of Siddhartha Gautama was his pragmatic and therapeutic approach. It was refreshing to find a teacher who wasn't interested in the question of God.

Does epistemology matter? The answer to that question is not epistemological, it's metaphysical. Immanuel Kant taught me that the most important questions are metaphysical. And it was David Hume, the Scottish philosopher, who, says Kant, awakened him from his dogmatic slumbers. Hume argued that reason isn't as important as we make it out to be. Ideas about justice, beauty or mathematics are merely human inventions. Causes *aren't* concrete things in the world, and neither are moral principles, and no amount of searching with the principles of logic or the tools of experience and experiment will reveal them. Kant took Hume's point. The rest is history. Kant constructed a philosophical system to rival that of Plato and Aristotle. Yes – another paradigm shift. This isn't the place to tell the story. But, as Susan Neiman says, what he set out to do was to show that the most important principles that govern our lives 'are not things we find in the world, but things we bring to it … principles [that] reside not in custom or habit, but in reason and understanding'.

The Enlightenment was about the overthrow of authority, tradition, monarchy, faith and privilege. It was the *ideas* – metaphysics – of Enlightenment philosophers like Kant that laid the foundations. They did so by propagating the ideas or concepts of tolerance, equality, democracy and individual freedom that led to the overthrow. Metaphysics can be revolutionary.

However, sometimes philosophy is best learned through humour. So, here are Cathcart and Klein about metaphysics:

DIMITRI: *Something's been bothering me lately, Tasso.*

TASSO: *What's that?*

DIMITRI: *What is the meaning of it all?*

TASSO: *All what?*

DIMITRI: *You know, life, death, love – the whole stuffed grape leaf.*

TASSO: *What makes you think any of it has any meaning?*

DIMITRI: *Because it has to. Otherwise life would just be …*

TASSO: *What?*

DIMITRI: *I need an ouzo.*

Reclaiming reverence

Whereof one cannot speak,
thereof one must remain silent.
– Ludwig Wittgenstein

I first met John Cumpsty some forty years ago. He was the newly appointed professor and head of the Department of Religious Studies at the University of Cape Town – an appointment made after a fierce debate about whether UCT should have a department of Theology or one of Religious Studies. The argument that won the day was that it was not appropriate for a university to teach theology 'from faith to faith', so to speak. Teaching religion in its own terms as a significant part of human history and experience was appropriate for a university.

I was then a Methodist minister sent to interview John for the Methodist newspaper *Dimension*. I was immediately struck by his depth, humanity and vision for Religious Studies at UCT. We found that we had a common interest in Reinhold Niebuhr. Thus began a forty-year friendship with John. I became his first PhD student and later joined the Religious Studies staff. I owe to John more than I can ever tell. He remained a stalwart of Religious Studies at UCT when I became involved in university management. (When I became vice chancellor at the University of Natal, I got a note of congratulations from John with one word – 'Wow.')

John Cumpsty brought to his scholarship as a teacher/researcher a breadth of experience seldom seen in academia. He was a trained engineer, with experience in the UK and USA. He was a barrister, and he was an ordained Anglican priest and theologian. John brought clarity of thought; he was not just a thinker, he was thoughtful. He opened things up. He met his postgraduate students where they were and nurtured them from there. He used to say 'write as though you were trying to communicate with a twelve-year-old' – and he did it himself. John was a big man physically – larger than life. His physical presence lingers; hair somewhat untidy, those awful brown pants he wore – he had little dress sense. Attending John's lectures was like watching tennis. He would start his sentence loud and end soft, so that listeners had to lean forward to catch his words. And, he would, mid-sentence, sniff left/right in his characteristic way.

One of my treasured memories of John is of me acting as his *handlanger* (assistant), mixing concrete to fill and screed a floor in our first house in Pinelands. John was a competent carpenter, bricklayer, plumber – you name it. He virtually rebuilt the successive houses he lived in. I can recall discussing a draft chapter of my thesis with John Cumpsty up a step ladder ...

John was above all a teacher and mentor. I think it was Aristotle who said, 'teaching is the highest form of learning'. John taught well because he grappled with the issues. He showed a remarkable confidence in his students, raising the bar constantly. He wrote *Religion as Belonging: A General Theory of Religion* (1991) because he wanted to explain to his students where he had got to in his intellectual pilgrimage.

Sadly, John finally succumbed to Alzheimer's disease. I still recall our last real conversation, over a pizza on a sunny day. 'If I were not committed to the Abrahamic family of religions', he said, reflecting on his spiritual journey, 'I think I might have become a Buddhist.'

That made sense because he had an uncanny knack of getting to the roots of a religious tradition. 'We owe our sense of *goals or ends*, of teleology', he would say, 'to the emphasis of the Abrahamic traditions on a transcendent God and a secular world.'

John published *Religion as Belonging* some years before he retired. It was a landmark book because he sought to develop a comparative theory of religion in its own terms, not a philosophy or history of religions.

Judaism, Christianity and Islam are 'Secular-World-Affirming-Religions' in John's terms. God is radically transcendent and the world is thoroughly secular. Time is linear and directional. Our modern notions of purpose and progress can be traced back to this view of time and history. Experience is tested in terms of goals, and human beings engage with the world out there, shaping it according to their needs.

Goals I understand; I've been called goal-driven. And in an organisational context that's usually taken as a compliment; executives should be 'driven', single-mindedly pursuing the objectives of the organisation.

The West owes much to the secular world-affirming religions; I doubt modern science and technology would have been possible without them. Indeed, Western thought, to which I am heir, has always subjected life to conceptual categories, to questions about meaning and about ends. And in its anxiety about meaning it has forgotten simply to experience the, according to John, 'texture' of life.

In John's book, Hinduism and Buddhism are examples of 'Withdrawal Religions', emphasising non-attachment. Time is cyclical, with the present texture emphasised. Human beings aspire to 'withdraw' from affective attachment. Here, I think John got it wrong. The texts and resources he drew upon at the time he wrote were dated. He admitted that his characterisation of Asian religious traditions as religions of 'withdrawal' was controversial.

Today we have access to sharper resources. Buddhism and Taoism are not about withdrawal. They are renunciate traditions that appreciate the texture of this world for what it is.

Appreciating the 'texture' is something I've had to learn. But it was not until I discovered Taoist/Chinese thought that I began to recognise the value of texture as the art of 'making this life significant', as the subtitle of Ames and Hall's translation and commentary of the *Dao De Jing* proclaims.

When I first read it, I truly felt the three D's – discombobulated, disturbed and disconcerted. It was a bit like I felt on a visit to Moscow in 1990; I wondered why I felt physically disorientated until I realised it was the absence of the visual stimulus of billboards and neon lights. Moscow was cold and grey. There simply was no advertising, and my sense of deprivation was disturbing.

My experience when first encountering the *Dao De Jing* was similar. Here was a strangely different worldview from the one that I, as an heir of the Judeo-Christian tradition, knew. The *Dao De Jing* originated in China during what is called the Warring States Period, between 403 and 221 BCE.

Taoists were different from anything I had thus far encountered. For one thing, they had no concept of 'cosmos' in the Greek sense. The Greek notion of the cosmos, so familiar to Westerners, conjures up a sense of a 'single-ordered Divine universe governed by natural and moral laws that are ultimately intelligible to the human mind' (Ames and Hall). For Taoists there is no 'beginning' to explain what follows in the universe. Space and time are interdependent.

Judeo-Christian tradition affirms that an all-powerful God makes things and commands the world into being. Taoists have no sense of *creatio ex nihilo*, of a Creator God who brings something into being out of nothing.

Taoists believe that life is made up of the things that constitute our experience. There is no view from nowhere, no vantage point from which we can view life. We are all in the soup. The upshot of this radical perspective, write Ames and Hall, is that 'each particular element in our experience is holographic ...' This is the idea that there is a universe in a grain of sand (William Blake). As Ames and Hall say, for Taoists 'there is an intoxicating bottomlessness to any particular event in our experience. The entire universe resides happily in the smile on the dirty face of this one little child.' We all affect each other. As chapter fourteen of the *Dao De Jing* puts it, cultivate personal excellence and you enhance the ethos of the world:

Cultivate it in your person,
And the character you develop will be genuine;
Cultivate it in your family,
And its character will be abundant;
Cultivate it in your village,
And its character will be enduring;
Cultivate it in the state,
And its character will flourish;
Cultivate it in the world,
And its character will be all-pervading.

Getting the most out of your experience requires a stewardship of your resources – nurturing them and using them frugally.

Entering the worldview of the Taoist is a novel experience for Westerners. We discover that we are not passive participants in our experience, going along for the ride, sometimes on autopilot. There is simply no appeal to some external efficient cause; no Creator God or primordial determinative principle that we can appeal to or blame. There is no pre-ordained design imposed upon us. Context is everything. We are where we are. We are challenged to get the most out of the ingredients of our lives.

François Jullien, a leading interpreter of the Taoist/Chinese way, illustrates the difference between Eastern and Western thought using the notion of happiness. Since Aristotle, he argues, human existence has depended on happiness – it's a universal goal – though there's little agreement about what constitutes happiness. The Chinese 'barely developed the idea of finality' (goal) and consequently 'showed ... little interest in happiness'. The word 'goal' had to be translated into modern Chinese to deal with the West.

In place of the Greek notion of *telos* (end or goal), Chinese thought emphasised what Jullien calls 'being in phase'. Success is not measured against some aim or goal, but by what might be called 'adequacy': 'A shoe is adequate if it makes us forget the foot. A belt is adequate if it makes us forget the waist ... Let adequacy begin and nonadequacy cease and you achieve adequacy that makes you forget adequacy.' So, once we have given up goals and the burdens that go with them, *'life itself* decides how it will go'. Imagine a world in which we are, to use Jullien's words, 'exempt from happiness'. We no longer feel we ought to be happy, and that something is wrong if we are not.

Adequacy, as an ancient Taoist sage says, is like a mirror. 'The accomplished man uses his spirit as a mirror ... The virtue of the mirror is that it accepts but does not hold: it reflects *everything* it encounters but allows things to *pass by* without clinging to them. It does not reject or retain. It allows things to appear and disappear without clinging to them.'

Here's the paradox, at least to Westerners. Goals are nothing; texture is everything. But we are encouraged not to cling to anything.

In recent years, there has been a spate of books on the theme of 'living without gods'. The general idea is that secularisation doesn't have to equate to joining the ranks of the new atheists who seem intent on seeing religion off the planet. Rather, those who no longer find it possible to believe in God or gods can live meaningfully, morally and joyfully without the consolations and costs of religion.

For example, the literary scholar George Lewis Levine has edited a book called *The Joy of Secularism: 11 Essays for How We Live Now* (2011). Many take the view that the world is to be explained and understood in natural terms. Put simply, 'it works always and everywhere without miracles or supernatural interventions'. Can we feel at home in such a world? What does this entail? Eleven contributors have a go at answering these questions.

This book is my go at this question. 'Secular spirituality' is not an exercise in nostalgia for things lost, a lament for what we can no longer believe. It's not a negative project, nor a wistful 're-enchanting' of the world. Weber described living in a disenchanted world as being trapped in an 'iron cage'. I don't see it that way. Well, then, how do I see it?

First, I want to be clear about how I use the word 'secular'. I think most secularists would agree with the way Philip Kitcher explains it. Secularists 'doubt the existence of the deities, divinities, spirits, ghosts, and ancestors, the sacredness of specific places, and the supernatural forces to which the world's various religions, past and present, make their varied appeals'. The world works everywhere and always without supernatural interventions. This is the immanent frame through which we *all* experience the world. This is not to say that there are not special times, places and events when we experience signals of transcendence. Moments of illumination, disclosure, intuition, enlightenment, revelation, inspiration. Secularists just don't interpret these experiences the way a theist would, as somehow God-given.

'Secular spirituality' seems at first sight to be a paradox. I suppose that's because, for many Westerners, the only socially observable spirituality for centuries has been a religion, specifically Christianity. We have come to think of spirituality and religion as the same thing. They are not. Look backwards to Greek spirituality or eastwards towards Taoism and Buddhism and you source a spirituality that is not religious in the sense of believing in God or gods.

But it was not until I discovered Paul Woodruff's book on reverence that I found a way of talking about secular spirituality.

Look up 'reverence' in the dictionary and you will find it defined as 'awe, respect, wonderment, surprise'. It's what you experience when you feel overcome, struck dumb by something that seems too sublime to be contained in our language. The birth of a child, a performance of Handel's *Messiah*, a sunset over the sea, a walk in the forest … It's what we mean by the word ineffable – something indescribable, beyond words. It's the feeling Wittgenstein expressed in his famous saying, 'Whereof one cannot speak, thereof one must be silent.'

Paul Woodruff is a philosopher and classicist. His book *Reverence: Renewing a Forgotten Virtue* (2001) is the only one of its kind in the English language, as far as I know. In ancient Greece and in ancient China, reverence was an important virtue, a way of being human and of being a leader. Strangely, although we have the word 'reverence' in our language, we hardly know how to use it. But I think secular spirituality needs it. Well, what is it? Let Woodruff speak for himself:

> Reverence begins in a deep understanding of human limitations; from this grows the capacity to be in awe of whatever we believe lies outside our control – God, truth, justice, nature, even death ... Simply put, reverence is the virtue that keeps human beings from trying to act like gods.

Reverence is that part of me that is able to see the universe in a grain of sand, to be able to crack a joke. It is not something I have made up because I can't make up (imagine, think about) anything without it.

What distinguishes reverence from religion? Religion, as ordinarily understood by most Westerners, involves dogma and belief in God, the supernatural or the sacred in some form. You will find expressions of reverence in all religions, but not all forms of reverence are religious.

For me, reverence lies at the heart of secular spirituality. It's the affirmation that we are finite beings who are open to infinity, transitory beings who are open to that which is ongoing, relative beings open to the unconditional. These metaphysical statements are not empirically demonstrable. They are statements about our inherent, yes, natural spirituality.

I think we are by nature spiritual beings. We do need, it seems, to feel connected to that which is 'larger' than us. Secular spirituality is not a sickness of the soul; it is not a negation of our human-ness. But, you don't have to belong to one or other religion to be spiritual.

That's a choice I make. And it's uniquely modern. Like reverence, virtue is a word we hardly use today. It even sounds quaint, a bit old-fashioned, and seems to suggest an attitude of self-righteousness, even priggishness. But in ancient Greece and China, reverence was a virtue you learned by practising it, cultivating it and nurturing it. And, says Woodruff, 'You'll never learn virtue unless you already know it'. You cannot be tone-deaf when it comes to reverence. The ancients believed that human beings are born with the capacity for reverence. They believed that reverence increases when it is cultivated in communities, in leaders and in family members.

Protagoras of ancient Greece invented a myth in which the highest god gave reverence and justice to human beings as a means for the survival of society. Why reverence and not just justice? Because Protagoras understood what the poets have been teaching, that justice is not enough.

Importantly, reverence is not the same thing as respect. As Woodruff points out, you can have too much respect and you can have respect for the wrong things. Respect is something you feel. Reverence is the capacity to have feelings. It i s not simply a feeling itself. That is why it's called a virtue. Something you can develop, nurture, cultivate – practise.

Remember that you are human; this is the central message of Greek reverence. You forget your humanity when you take on the airs like a god, lording it over others, or when you act like a beast of prey, raping, pillaging, killing and exploiting.

How do I cultivate the virtue of reverence? Mindfully, I think. The opposite of mindful reverence? Self-absorption or self-importance. To speak of self-reverence is to speak nonsense. Mindful meditation enables me to practise the virtue of reverence. And why? Because, the ancients affirmed, if I have the capacity for reverence, I am more likely to make the right choices when confronted with the need to act.

I am aware that I have not emphasised sufficiently the importance of institutions. And it's been bothering me. What would be the institutional expression of 'secular spirituality'?

It's a strange blind spot for one trained in the social sciences. Modernity is the story of the founding of new institutions – the factory, the 24-hour shift, urbanisation, the nuclear family, the middle class and the nation state, to name a few.

Religion is *always* expressed in institutions. Durkheim defined religion as a set of beliefs that bound people into a moral community. Jews have their synagogues, Christians have their churches, and Muslims have their mosques.

Robert Bellah drew our attention to the way secular states like the USA appeal to the transcendent – to 'civil religion' – to bind people together and reinforce the authority of government. In my own family, our daughter, in her PhD dissertation, looked at the role of religion in the formation of South Africa's democratic constitution, and the way the ANC uses religion to foster social solidarity – its own brand of civil religion.

The word religion comes from the Latin noun '*religio*'. One etymology of '*religio*' says it comes from the verb '*religare*', which, as we have seen, means 'to bind'. Religion is that which binds people with common beliefs and practices. Another etymology has *religio* deriving from the verb '*relegare*', which means 'to contemplate' or 'to re-read'. On this reading, religion describes the myths, founding texts and rituals of a particular tradition. When you put both meanings together, *religion is that which binds people together in a particular faith-tradition, which is defined by its myths and symbols, its founding texts and its rituals.*

One of the challenges to what I'm calling 'secular spirituality' is that it has no such community of practice.

What might be surprising is the current resurgence of religion worldwide. The dangerous interdependence between politics and religion is also once again on the increase. This situation has left social theorists puzzling over two different but related questions.

The first has to do with what provides legitimacy to a modern secular state. Such a state is a popular sovereignty, the rule of the people by the people. And they govern, or are governed, through the rule of law. The question is: What gives the law authority? Why should anyone obey the law? In a secular state, the people cede to the legislators the authority they need to exercise sanctions over those who refuse to obey the laws of the land. This thoroughly secular view of politics suffers from a major drawback, one that has been particularly telling in the South African context. What happens when people don't recognise the legitimacy of the courts and the constitution to uphold the rule of law? When the call is to make things ungovernable?

The other puzzling question has to do with the role of religion in politics. When politics is undergirded by appeals to divine will, religion provides the motivational set of moral imperatives that binds the people and gives politics its legitimacy. In its weak form the monarchy and the Established Church in England combine to give the polity its legitimacy. England has a mild form of civil religion. In its strong form, you have a theocracy – a form of 'government by God or god directly or through a priestly order' of some sort, as in the case of Iran.

Despite its legitimation issues, I favour a strong secular state, where church and state are separated, where religion and politics are not interdependent.

I cannot envisage a functional alternative to the 'church' for those who practise a 'secular spirituality'. Almost certainly they will be found in secular organisations where they share what might be called a 'fellowship of agreed principles' – a community of practice.

Can you be moral without God? Can you be a loving person, can you love justice, if you don't believe in God? Are ethical claims upon us meaningless and unjustified without belief in God?

It's true that religion has undergirded ethics through the ages. Put another way, human beings have enshrined their deepest values in their religions. And they have gone on to say that what is good, what is of value, is what the deities have willed.

Many people believe that unless we believe in God we are unlikely to act morally. Voltaire (1694–1778), the French philosopher and atheist, refused to allow his friends to discuss atheism in front of his servants, saying: 'I want my lawyer, tailor, valets, even my wife to believe in God. I think that if they do I shall be robbed less and cheated less'.

The argument that you cannot be a good, loving, compassionate human being if you don't believe in God is not new. It's a debate that goes back at least to Plato and Socrates. Those who thought that ethics was impossible without God reasoned in two ways. Some argued that the good was defined by what God willed. Others took the view that God reveals the good to us, good that we cannot know independently.

Plato pointed out the flaw in these arguments when he asked: Are things wrong because God says so? Or, does God say they are wrong because they are?

Let's take the second question. If something is wrong, it is wrong – it doesn't need God to make it so. The first question is tougher. Surely we don't believe that some things are wrong because God says so? In some traditions 'thou shalt not kill' is a God-given commandment. Does that mean that prior to God's decree killing wasn't wrong? Surely not. Morality, as Stephen Law says, 'is ultimately independent of both our own will and God's too'.

Will we be good, responsible human beings – whether or not we are believers? That's a different question. And one that has plagued me. Is the Dalai Lama right when he says, 'whether a person is a religious believer or not does not matter much? Far more important is that they be good human beings' (*Beyond Religion: Ethics for the Whole World*, 2011). Why should we be good, responsible human beings? This too is an age-old question. Hans Jonas has helped me to craft some sort of answer.

◇ For the first time in human history, we have the technological means to kill the world. Our actions today do affect our unborn neighbours of tomorrow.

◇ This lengthened reach of our deeds moves *responsibility* into the centre of the ethical stage.

◇ We can no longer act with impunity – without regard to consequences.

◇ The state of available information (data) will always be incomplete. This, and our inability to predict the future, means we must resort to 'the heuristics of fear' (Hans Jonas) rather than to hopeful projections. It is possible that we will kill the world. We must therefore sharpen what Berger calls the 'calculus of pain' and extend it to include the natural world, Planet Earth.

◇ The ecological imperative is to treat the natural order as an *end* and not as a means for gratifying our consumerist appetites.

◇ We need to develop a new understanding of humankind, one that is embedded in nature.

◇ It is imperative that we develop an ethics of responsibility that is thoroughly secular and compelling.

175

Karen Armstrong and the Dalai Lama have recently published stirring appeals for a return to compassion and ethics to alleviate the immense suffering in our world of plenty.

When the ex-nun and historian of religions Karen Armstrong won the TED prize of $100 000, plus the means to make a wish for a better world come true, she said she knew immediately what she wanted: 'One of the chief tasks of our time must surely be to build a global community in which all peoples can live together in mutual respect.' She asked TED to assist her to create, launch and propagate a Charter for Compassion. The aim of the Charter would be to 'restore compassion to the heart of religious and moral life' to counter the 'voices of extremism, intolerance and hatred'.

Many people from around the world contributed to a draft charter, and a group of notable individuals from six faith traditions (Judaism, Christianity, Islam, Hinduism, Buddhism and Confucianism) helped to compose the final version. It's worth reproducing the Charter, which has been translated into over thirty languages:

⋄ The principle of compassion lies at the heart of all religious, ethical, and spiritual traditions, calling us always to treat all others as we would be treated ourselves.

⋄ Compassion impels us to work tirelessly to alleviate the suffering of our fellow creatures, to dethrone ourselves from the centre of our world and put others there, and to honour the inviolable sanctity of every single human being, treating everybody, without exception, with absolute justice, equity and respect.

⋄ It is also necessary in both public and private life to refrain consistently and empathetically from inflicting pain. To act or speak violently out of spite, chauvinism or self-interest, to impoverish, exploit or deny basic rights to anybody, and incite hatred by denigrating others – even our enemies – is a denial of our common humanity.

⋄ We acknowledge that we have failed to live compassionately and that some have even increased the sum of human misery in the name of religion.

We therefore call upon all men and women:

⋄ To restore compassion to the centre of morality and religion.
⋄ To return to the ancient principle that any interpretation of

scripture that breeds violence, or disdain is illegitimate.

◇ To ensure that youth are given accurate and respectful information about other traditions, religions and cultures.

◇ To encourage a positive appreciation of cultural and religious diversity.

◇ To cultivate an informed empathy with the suffering of all human beings – even those regarded as enemies.

We urgently need to make compassion a clear, luminous and dynamic force in our polarised world. Rooted in a principled determination to transcend selfishness, compassion can break down political, dogmatic, ideological and religious boundaries.

Born of our deep interdependence, compassion is essential to human relationships and to a fulfilled humanity. It is the path to enlightenment, and indispensable to the creation of a just economy, and a peaceful global economy.

I can't help but be deeply moved by this ringing call to compassion addressed, mainly, to the faith traditions. But Armstrong doesn't leave it there. Her book, *Twelve Steps to a Compassionate Life* (2010), provides a practical twelve-step programme. She believes that we can 're-train our responses and form mental habits that are kinder, gentler, and less fearful of others'. We can, in short, become more compassionate people.

Writing for a different public from that of Armstrong, the Dalai Lama has called for secular ethics. In the face of the dire challenges of our time he says: 'What we need today is an approach to ethics which makes no recourse to religion and can be equally acceptable to those with faith and those without: a secular ethics.' For someone who has been a Buddhist monk since the age of six, it's a surprising call. And it stems from his belief that in today's world any religion-based ethics which attempts to address our 'neglect of inner values can never be universal' (*Beyond Religion*).

Secular ethics for the Dalai Lama must be founded on 'inner

values' – 'qualities that we all appreciate in others, and toward which we all have a natural instinct, bequeathed by our biological nature as animals that survive and thrive only in an environment of concern, affection, and warmheartedness – or in a single word, compassion'. And the essence of compassion is a wish to alleviate the suffering of others and promote their wellbeing. This is 'the spiritual principle from which all other positive inner values emerge'.

In the first part of the book, the Dalai Lama lays the groundwork for a secular ethics that individuals can subscribe to, whether or not they belong to a faith-tradition. Born in 1935 in a small village in Tibet, he has spent much of his life as a stateless refugee in India. Reflecting on his life and times, he says there is much to rejoice about – medical science has improved health, millions have been lifted out of poverty, been educated, enjoy human rights and live in democracies. But, despite our advances, there is still great suffering, and humankind faces enormous challenges.

'Ultimately', writes the Dalai Lama, 'the source of our problems lies at the level of the individual. If people lack moral values and integrity, no system of laws and regulations will be adequate. So long as people give priority to material values, then injustice, corruption, inequity, intolerance, and greed – all the outward manifestations of neglect of inner values – will persist'.

Where are we to turn to for help? Science, for all its benefits, cannot provide the grounding for inner values. What we need is 'a new secular approach to universal ethics'. This is the Dalai Lama's bold call.

The Dalai Lama sets out a 'new vision of secular ethics'. It draws on his conversations with scientists, leaders, and ordinary people over the years. It's not difficult, he says, to demonstrate – without recourse to religion – that:

◇ we share a common humanity;
◇ we all seek happiness;

◇ compassion is the foundation of wellbeing or happiness;

◇ compassion underwrites our search for justice;

◇ non-violence rather than an escalation in violence is in our interests; and

◇ we need a common ethics for our shared world.

Then he calls for '[e]ducating the heart through training the mind'. How are we to become more compassionate, kinder, forgiving, and more discerning in our behaviour? We can do so, says the Dalai Lama, by 'training the mind' to 'restrain our negative behaviour', 'combat our destructive emotional tendencies' and 'cultivate inner values such as compassion, patience, contentment, self-discipline, and generosity'. We can develop a calm and disciplined mind through 'mental training'.

He draws on classical Buddhist traditions of 'mind training', called *lojong* in Tibetan, which place meditation at their centre. He emphasises that these practices require no religious belief or commitment, but they do constitute a way of living ethically in harmony with others – compassionately.

There is a clear convergence in these recent calls from Karen Armstrong and the Dalai Lama. Earlier, I referred to John F. Kennedy's observation that for the first time in human history we have the means to feed the world. What we lack, according to Armstrong and the Dalai Lama, is compassion toward those who are hungry. The challenge to love unconditionally, to be compassionate, is to be found in all religious *and* secular value systems. We need morality because we cannot love or be compassionate without it.

But there is a certain naivety about the Charter of Compassion and about the Dalai Lama's secular ethics or 'inner values'. When Kennedy talked about feeding the hungry, what he actually said was that we lack the *will* to do so. And the will to feed the hungry must be expressed in political terms. Hunger is pre-eminently a political-economic matter. It's an issue for social ethics. And in matters of politics and economics compassion must be translated into justice.

If we have learned anything from modern social theory, it is the distinction between 'troubles' and 'issues', first made explicit by C. Wright Mills in *The Sociological Imagination* (1959). I will illustrate this distinction by citing a newspaper column by Mosibudi Mangena in the *Cape Times* (24 October 2012). Mangena is the leader of AZAPO and a former Minister of Science and Technology. I met him when he officially opened a science and maths centre at the University of Venda when I was acting vice chancellor. In his column, he tells of how distraught his wife and he were when two young Zimbabwean girls, aged about fifteen or sixteen, each with a baby on her back, knocked at their door looking for handouts to keep them alive. They had fled from hunger and poverty in Zimbabwe, the fathers of their babies had disappeared, and they slept in a shipping container.

Acting out of compassion, the Mangenas gave the girls what they could. This was an instance of indigent young women in 'trouble'. But, Mangena reflects how their troubles are part of a much larger 'issue' – the political and economic meltdown in Zimbabwe and growing unemployment in South Africa, which is itself experiencing serious economic and political problems.

If there were more Mangenas, the quantum of compassion shown to those who are unemployed and mired in poverty would surely grow. But that would not address the structural problems of the political meltdown and economic stagnation at the heart of the story of these two young girls. 'Everything begins in mysticism and ends in politics', said Charles Péguy, the French intellectual and activist. Put differently, love makes us sensitive to the needs of others. Politics is the arena where issues of poverty and unemployment must be addressed, and justice is how we evaluate political actions.

As Reinhold Niebuhr never ceased to remind us, 'in the process of building communities, every impulse of love must be transformed into an impulse for justice ... Justice means the calculation of rights.

It means taking sides for the weak against the strong. It means rational discrimination between competing claims'.

Niebuhr knew that the self-interest of all social groups is such that their power cannot be left unchecked, and that justice is about efforts to increase the power of the victims of injustice. Justice in human society rests on a balance of power. Democracy is the system, created after the spilling of much blood and the efforts of many, that allows for the endless balancing of competing interests.

In the words of Niebuhr's famous dictum: 'Man's capacity for justice makes democracy possible; but his inclination to injustice makes democracy necessary'. Writing towards the end of the Second World War, Niebuhr points out that in all 'non-democratic political theories the state or the ruler is invested with uncontrolled power for the sake of achieving order … irresponsible and uncontrolled power is the greatest source of injustice'.

Sadly the girls who knocked on the Mangenas' door will not know a better life until the abuses of power in Zimbabwe end and the economy recovers. Neither will they get a fair deal in South Africa if the politics of patronage and corruption continue.

Compassion will make us all more sensitive to the needs and the plight of others. But compassion cannot take the place of justice in society. And justice cannot prevail unless those who have access to power are checked by those who don't – in the space we call democracy. Secular spirituality with a healthy dose of compassion and political realism.

I'm aware that there's a touch of James the preacher in these remarks. So I unearthed some old sermons. How are the Rev. James's sermons different from what I'm saying now? In 1973, when I was teaching at Fedsem, I preached a sermon about my difficulties with orthodoxy, especially concerning the doctrine of God. Words like 'omnipotence' and 'omniscience' portray a complacent being who has got everything and needs nothing. 'I believe in a God who wants things,' I said. He wants people to enjoy his world. And, in the words of the prophet Micah, he wants us 'to act justly, to love mercy, to walk humbly with him' (Micah 6:8).

How to marry compassion and justice, faced as we are by unprecedented moral and political challenges? What, for example, does acting justly and mercifully mean in a world where the USA and the UK are escalating the use of drones in their war against terror?

Forty-six years later, the James of 2021 no longer believes in the God of orthodoxy. But I still believe it is imperative that we act justly, love mercy and walk humbly, reverently in the face of the challenges of our time. My poem on reverence tries to capture this.

> If you can't feel it,
> have your spirit soar
> at the sound of birdsong
> or the cry of a newborn baby.
>
> If you can't see it in the majestic mountain;
> Or the smile on the grubby face of a child;
> Or the artistry of Michelangelo's David;
> Or the beauty of your beloved;
>
> You will not feel reverence
> nor understand why we
> need today to reclaim
> this ancient virtue.
>
> It's the Something that
> makes you a lover of art;
> The Something that the scientist feels
> on the cusp of a breakthrough.

Reverence is what the statesperson feels
in the face of the ideal of justice.

Reverence is prior to
religion and spirituality.
It's the Something that fills me
with awe and wonder.
The Something I feel when
I'm shamed by my uncaring.
Reverence is ineffable,
it refuses to be captured.
Like love, it can't be willed
but you know it
when you feel it.

I vow to cultivate
the reverence I was born with.
To practice the ancient virtue
of reverence mindfully.

Interlude

I wonder if memory is true,
and I know that it cannot be,
but that one lives by memory nonetheless
and not by truth.
– Igor Stravinsky

Writing in his old age, the composer Igor Stravinsky offers us his understanding of memory. Certainly we live as though it were true. 'Memory is identity', writes Julian Barnes. 'I have believed that since – oh, since I can remember'. Anyone who has lost a loved one to Alzheimer's disease knows that they have gone off to a world that only they know. When we lose our memories we lose ourselves; we are not ourselves.

Memory assures us of our past. It enables me to reconstruct that past. But no matter how hard I try, I cannot live in the past or experience the past. As the mystics say, my memory 'is itself a present experience'. I can only know the past in the present, as part of the present. 'Anticipation, like memory, is a present fact', says Ken Wilber in *No Boundary: Eastern and Western Approaches to Personal Growth* (2001).

The seeds of my crisis of faith were sown when, at the tender age of eleven, I was profoundly shaken while watching that film of the liberation of the concentration camps.

That spectre has had a deep effect on me. It haunts the literature and social theory of my epoch too. We're not free to live and think as though it did not happen. The Holocaust stands as a symbol of the dark or shadow side of modernity. We know that science, technology and bureaucracy, even medicine, can be used to destroy as well as to uplift. The Holocaust calls into question our fondly held and taken-for-granted assumptions about humankind, God, evil, ideology, nuclear armaments, political power and social engineering.

Part of what we mean by modernity involves grappling with that unprecedented scale of suffering and death. Not only that, the Holocaust taught those in power that to execute massive social engineering all you need is a utopian ideology combined with modern technology and bureaucracy and you can contrive genocide. Millions of people died in Stalin's Russia, Mao's China, Pol Pot's Cambodia and Rwanda's genocide. Those of us who were born around the time of the Second World War have since witnessed purges, expulsions and terror-famines on a scale hitherto unimagined, even unimaginable – a surfeit of what Adi Ophir calls 'superfluous evil'.

I have the same feeling about the calamitous effects of global warming. Not only do we now have the capacity to kill the world but it seems that we are also intent on doing so.

What of the ever-present threat of nuclear war?

What of the alarming increase in the use of killer drones?

Are we about to enter a new cold war?

Those familiar with Marcus Zusak's novel, *The Book Thief* (2007), will recall the following story. Once upon a time, there was a Jew named Max who was given shelter by a German family, the Hubermanns, during the Nazi scourge. He had travelled many miles to this safe haven, enduring hardship and the ever-present danger of capture. Part of his disguise was to carry a copy of the Führer's *Mein Kampf* with him. At great risk to themselves, the Hubermanns made him welcome and hid him in their dank and airless cellar. Over time, Max won their friendship and that of Liesel, their young daughter.

As hostilities increased, so did the danger. Supplies dwindled. Hans, the head of the household, was a painter. But work was scarce. Lacking writing paper, Max cut out some pages from *Mein Kampf* and painted them white using the paint he found in the cellar. He found string and hung the pages up to dry. And when the pages were ready he wrote on them a story for Liesel called 'The

Standover Man'. The story began: 'All my life I've been scared of men standing over me'. First it was his father, then the bully at school and then, many years later, it was a friend who woke him when it was time for him to go to the Hubermanns. Then it was Hans Hubermann who stood over him when he awoke after three days of exhausted sleep. In his dreams, a shadowy figure hovers over him, possibly his captor. But, through it all he comes to realise that the best standover man is not a man at all – it is the friendship of young Liesel.

Living without gods is about living without a standover man, whether it be the Führer or the bully at school. Whether it be an all-powerful God or an authoritarian state. It's about taking responsibility rather than ceding it to someone or something else. It's about painting over the words, the ideas, the ideologies, the authority figures – everything that seeks to keep you in bondage.

It's about writing your own script. The parable of the standover man is also a reminder that it is possible to paint over that which hurts and destroys and to write a new story – one that our children and our children's children will rejoice in.

Critic Harold Bloom says that of all the poets of his time who wrote in English, Keats has revealed the most power to move readers in our day. John Keats's extraordinary life was cut short when he died of tuberculosis in 1821, at the age of twenty-three. There was a moment in his life when as a mere nineteen-year-old, he said:

several things dove-tailed in my mind, and at once it struck me what quality went to form a Man of Achievement, especially in Literature, and which Shakespeare possessed so enormously: I mean Negative Capability, that is, when a man is capable of being in uncertainties, mysteries, doubts, without any irritable reaching after fact and reason …

I'm no Keats, though I think that over the years I have developed some negative capability. It has not been easy; I was trained in the rational and empirical intellectual tradition of the West, which has given to the world calculative thinking. It's the thinking that has given us modern science and technology. I have had to learn to be in 'uncertainties, mysteries, doubts'. This is the contemplative thinking of which Heidegger also spoke.

Do not fall prey to the 'irritable reaching after fact and reason', said Keats. There is a time for *not*-doing. Living in a different key is *not* to strive for control, certainty, completeness, even comfort.

I think of the Stoics of ancient Greece – there are modern ones too – who practised negative capability. They taught that it's possible to choose not to be distressed by events, even if we can't choose the events themselves. This is the foundation of tranquillity.

Oliver Burkeman tells the story of a modern-day Stoic teacher and his wife in London. Keith and Jocelyn Seddon live in a simple cottage in Watford. Jocelyn is in her early fifties and suffers from rheumatoid arthritis. She has difficulty raising a glass to her lips. Keith is her carer and suffers from chronic fatigue syndrome. Both have PhDs and had planned academic careers, but then Jocelyn's illness arrived as an uninvited guest. Keith is now a tutor of correspondence courses in Stoicism, teaching students at private American universities. But the work is drying up – not much stomach for Stoicism in America – and money is tight.

But the mood in the Seddons' cottage is not despairing. Jocelyn seems serene; Keith, meanwhile, is 'practically bubbly', says Burkeman. The Seddons are witnesses to what Stoics teach. The 'only things we can control are our *judgements* – what we believe – about our circumstances … our judgements are what cause our distress … they're [what] we need to be able to control in order to substitute serenity for suffering.' In my own life, the practice of mindfulness meditation enables me to observe my thoughts and emotions as they arise, to see them as signposts rather than determinants of actions.

To return to John Keats: his appeal lies in his thoroughgoing naturalistic humanism, says Bloom. It allows him to embrace the world confidently. Then there is his 'extraordinary detachment', a capacity for bracketing his own interests to describe what he sees without flinching. Even the 'tragic acceptance' of what is, including the onset of tuberculosis.

Keats seemed to embody a secular spirituality. A humanism that is of this world, an ability to suspend one's judgments and see the moment for what it is, and the capacity to take the long view in the knowledge that the world will survive our perceptions of it.

I first came across the little-known word 'consilience' when I read Edward O. Wilson's fascinating book of the same title (1998). The renowned biologist, writing near the end of his career, borrowed the word from the philosophy of science to argue for a rethink in the face of the challenges of our time.

The fragmentation of knowledge, the balkanisation of intellectual disciplines, and the artificial boundaries between the sciences and the humanities 'are not reflections of the real world but artefacts of scholarship', he concluded. 'Consilience' means the jumping together of knowledge in the sciences. Can we hope for consilience across the great branches of learning? As in the CHEC library project, CALICO. And why would we want that? The problems that bedevil humankind can only be solved through consilience. Unless the sciences and the humanities work together we will not be able to address them.

And Wilson is right. Think of the HIV/Aids pandemic in South Africa, it's not just a challenge for the biologist and medical biochemist. Nor is it only a medical problem. The pandemic needs to be tackled with the combined resources of the sciences. But that alone will not suffice. HIV/Aids is also about values, virtues and human behaviour – the stuff of the humanities – sexuality, gender, human boundaries, death and more. Without consilience we will not win the battle against this pandemic. Think of any major public policy issue – from poverty, inequality and global warming to environmental degradation or most recently the Coronavirus pandemic – and you're looking at an issue that will require the combined efforts of the best brains in a multitude of disciplines. The tougher the issue, the more we need consilience.

For me, consilience is also a metaphor for drawing on the best traditions of therapy in the West and the East. The 'jumping together' of West and East. For example, Buddhists make a distinction between pain and suffering. Pain is to be expected, and most times we can't escape it. One of the miracles of modern palliative medicine is our ability to manage pain. As a young pastor, I witnessed the awful, unremitting pain of the terminally ill because pain management was in its infancy in those days. In contrast, suffering is optional because it is due to our attachments and our attempts to deny our mortality and impermanence. Buddhist and Stoic teaching on suffering and non-attachment to things is radical. It's about approaching all of life – inner thoughts and emotions as well as outer circumstances – without being hooked on them. Tibetan Buddhists even have a word for this sense of 'being hooked' – *shenpa*. Living without attachment or aversion.

It's a metaphor, too, for a secular spirituality that draws on both East and West …

'Philosophy as a way of life'

There is another world, but it is this one.
– Paul Éluard

The journey I've been describing in this book is about how my mind has changed over the years as I've wrestled with questions of faith, meaning and ethics. Questions prompted by the situations I've found myself in, and sometimes by the tools of philosophy and social theory I've been using. But always interaction between context and thought.

Heady stuff, you might say. But for me philosophy has never been merely an abstract and theoretical activity. In the world of the ancient Greeks and Romans, philosophy was emphatically not an abstract theoretical activity. It was, in the words of a leading classical scholar, Pierre Hadot, 'a method of training people to live and to look at the world in a new way'.

We often associate philosophy with using reason to pursue the abstract and unknown. But the Greek word philosophy means 'love of wisdom'. And this love of wisdom had a practical bent. It was about *how* to live meaningfully, ethically and wisely. As mentioned before, ancient schools of philosophy devised 'spiritual exercises' to help people to *practice* the good life. Exercises such as asking questions and not accepting things at face value, reading, listening, paying attention, meditating, and learning how to die.

The philosophical schools in the Greco-Roman world, like the Stoics and the Epicureans, understood philosophy as a *therapeutic* tool. You belonged to one of these schools because you had become convinced that human suffering can be overcome by practicing a way of life that involved exercises in right thinking and right living.

So whether, like Socrates, you're interested in the pursuit of self-knowledge, or like Aristotle, you're interested in the pursuit of 'human flourishing', or like Plato, you want to know what 'Good' is – these ancient philosophers had practical ways of showing you *how*. The two-thousand-five-hundred-year-old tradition of Western philosophy, it turns out, is about developing the therapeutic practice of wisdom in pursuit of the good life.

You may ask, why do we need therapy? What ails humankind? Well, says Hadot, according to all Greco-Roman schools of philosophy 'mankind's principal cause of suffering, disorder, and unconsciousness were the passions: ... unregulated desires and exaggerated fears'.

Remember that in Greek thought passions were *emotions* – like fear, greed or anger. And, unlike other types of feelings, these emotions involve beliefs. I feel fear because I believe something is likely to cause me pain or harm, or in some other way to be threatening. I fear something because I believe it to be dangerous in some way. Emotions like fear are to some extent subject to rational guidance. If I can change my perception of danger – that it's less dangerous than I thought – I can become less fearful.

In other words, we need a therapy for the passions or emotions to educate us and create in us new habits – to learn how to live well without being a slave to our fear or anger. Modern cognitive therapies work on the same principle.

The '*gymnasion*', to use the original Greek word, was the place where the philosophical schools worked at self-formation through physical and spiritual training. Much like athletes work out at the gym to improve and strengthen their bodies, people were encouraged to do 'spiritual exercises' to strengthen their souls and modify their behaviour. Self-transformation was the goal of the philosophical gymnasium.

What I find so interesting is that in the East thousands of years ago Siddhartha Gautama was developing a similar approach!

Recent scholarship on the roots of Buddhism show that the Buddha was not engaged in developing a worldview or philosophy that bettered that of the Hinduism of his day. He refrained from metaphysical speculation. As we have seen, he refused to address the big metaphysical questions: Is the world eternal or not? Is there life after death?

Rather than getting embroiled in these debates, he taught a therapeutic and pragmatic eight-fold path that went to the heart of why we suffer and *how* we can lead more meaningful and fruitful lives. The eightfold path: right understanding, right intention, right speech, right action, right livelihood, right effort, right mindfulness and right meditation. The Buddha's method, it turns out, was not that different from the early Greco-Roman philosophers. It was therapeutic, practical – he taught a '*praxis*'. A fine word that goes back to Aristotle and means voluntary or goal-directed activity, ethical in content and designed to enable a person to live meaningfully and well.

Where the West and the East differed was on what ails humankind.

For the early Greeks, humankind was subject to passions and interests. But they believed that people can be trained to develop moral virtues. People can learn how to overcome fear or greed or cowardice. How to temper their self-interest. Without such training society itself would not be possible.

Being consumed by passions or harmful emotions is something we understand in South Africa. Our incidence of rape and abuse of women are among the worst in the world – sex crimes that are essentially about power and domination. Over the ten Zuma years, our state-owned enterprises have been plundered in an orgy of state capture by people in positions of power and responsibility who are consumed by greed. The greed continues. Indeed, South Africans have come to fear for our fragile democracy. The Greeks understood that society itself is endangered when people are consumed by passions and by unbridled self-interest.

In the interests of the good life, of the common good, Greek philosophy taught the cultivation of 'virtues' or life skills. Virtues are habits that can be learned like any other skill – playing the violin or riding a bicycle. You learn to be kind by acts of kindness, you learn to become fair-minded by acting fairly, you learn to be self-controlled by not giving vent to your anger.

The East had a different take. For the Buddha, what ails humankind is suffering or *dukkha*. In a famous discourse, he teaches that suffering is all-embracing. 'Birth is *dukkha*, aging is dukkha, sickness is *dukkha*, death is *dukkha*'. But that's not the end of it, 'encountering what is not dear is *dukkha*, separation from what is dear is *dukkha*, not getting what one wants is *dukkha*'.

All these forms of attachment or clinging are what cause our existential suffering. Like a physician, having made his diagnosis the Buddha turns immediately to the therapy. Greed must be transformed into generosity, ill will into compassion and delusion into wisdom. The remedy for what ails humankind is a set of exercises, the eightfold path, the practice of which will overcome suffering. And he often uses artisanal metaphors: the farmer irrigating his field or the carpenter shaping a piece of wood.

Whether you look to the West or to the East, philosophy is about getting your head and your heart right through practice. Philosophy turns out to be *a way of life* that embodies all of what it is to be human – our bodies, our minds and our emotions.

Four vows are recited in Zen monasteries daily. They are vows of the *Bodhisattva* – the person who is committed to live for others. I want to give my own interpretation of these vows and use them as a framework for this concluding chapter. I also draw inspiration from Antony Osler's beautifully written meditation called *Stoep Zen* (2008). He's a South African, Zen Buddhist monk, human rights lawyer and Karoo farmer.

The first is a vow *to reduce suffering in the world*. The second is *to drop the endless delusions* we are prone to. The third is *to walk the dharma path* to meaning and goodness ('*dharma*' being a Sanskrit word which can be translated as the path of wisdom and enlightenment).

194

The fourth vow is *to recognise that ultimate reality is inconceivable –* beyond our grasp.

Imagine yourself training to reach a level of fitness, even skilfulness, where you are committed to reducing levels of human suffering rather than adding to them. Where you are mindful enough to spot your delusions when they occur and to drop them. Where you follow *dharma* paths of meaning and goodness, wherever they lead. And where you exercise a degree of humility and modesty in your quest for truth and meaning. That's philosophy as a way of life.

> *I VOW TO REDUCE HUMAN SUFFERING*
> *The Buddha tells us to look life straight in the eye,*
> *not to avoid or wish it away… In practice this vow*
> *means to give ourselves away to whoever is in front of us.*
> *Antony Osler in* Stoep Zen

There are those who argue that reason, science and social justice have brought about a world in which there is *less* human suffering, there are fewer wars and more peace than ever before. Steven Pinker is a leading proponent of such a view of the sweep of history. His two recent books, *The Better Angels of our Nature* (2011) and *Enlightenment Now* (2018), make for compelling reading. He writes in the latter:

> The Enlightenment principle that we can apply reason and sympathy to enhance human flourishing may seem obvious … it is not. More than ever, the ideals of reason, science, humanism, and progress need wholehearted defence.

Using big data, Pinker amasses an impressive array of evidence which shows a discernible downward trend in violence in the world. He also makes the case that all the usual indicators of human wellbeing – longevity, health, sustenance, wealth-generation and reducing inequality, safety and security, democracy, human rights, quality of life and even happiness – are better than they have ever been.

But Pinker is no supporter of the ideology of the inevitability of progress. As he says in *Enlightenment Now*, 'we will never live in a perfect world, and it would be dangerous to seek one. But there is no limit to the betterments we can attain if we continue to apply knowledge to enhance human flourishing.'

As long as there is human suffering in the world, as long as planet Earth is threatened, it is imperative that we seek to reduce suffering wherever we find it. And much of that suffering is what Adi Ophir calls 'superfluous'; unnecessary suffering inflicted by humans on others.

You may recall C. Wright Mills's distinction between 'troubles' and 'issues'. Previously, I illustrated this distinction by citing a *Cape Times* newspaper column by Mosibudi Mangena. The plight of the two Zimbabwean girls can be described as an instance of superfluous evil wrought by human society on these young mothers.

The vow to reduce human suffering will need to bear this distinction in mind. Hunger and unemployment are socio-economic and political issues that bedevil many countries. Confronted by these issues, compassionate concern for the poor and jobless must be translated into ways of achieving social justice. And, dare I say, some healthy utopian thinking.

Let me explain. For most of my adult life I've been a forager – looking for ideas that throw light on my life and times, for ways to solve the issues of the day. And occasionally I am *really* excited about a book. Rutger Bregman's *Utopia for Realists* (2014) is such a book. Bregman is a Dutch historian and journalist who at age thirty had four books to his name. He belongs to a new generation of thinkers who are breaking the mould and suggesting new and exciting alternatives to the tired orthodoxies that haven't proven very effective in the face of persistent problems like poverty, mechanisation, unemployment and homelessness.

He reminds us that Thomas More wrote *the* book on utopia and coined the term (*Utopia*, 1516). For More, utopia was an indictment on the greedy aristocracy that demanded more luxury as common people lived in extreme poverty. Utopias, says Bregman, 'throw open the windows of the mind'. We need 'a new lodestar, a new map of the world that once again includes a distant, unchartered continent – Utopia'. 'What we need are alternative horizons that spark the imagination'. Alternative horizons that give us a glimpse of a world where poverty, unemployment and mechanisation are tackled with vision and courage.

As Steven Pinker says of Bregman's book on its cover: 'If you're bored with hackneyed debates, decades-old right-wing and left-wing clichés, you may enjoy the bold thinking, fresh ideas, lively prose, and evidence-based arguments in *Utopia for Realists*.'

Bregman definitely does not have his head in the clouds. He marshals compelling evidence from peer-reviewed research to back his arguments. When I read Bregman, I was reminded of Peter Berger's call years ago, in 1974, for 'hard-nosed' analysis and a 'utopian' imagination. In the face of the problems that beset us on the southern tip of the African continent we need both.

The vow to reduce human suffering demands nothing less.

I VOW TO DROP MY DELUSIONS
A delusion is ...when we look at life through the distortions of
ignorance, prejudice, resistance, fear, anger,
avoidance, expectation, resentment, guilt.
Antony Osler in Stoep Zen

Psychologists like to distinguish illusions from delusions. Illusions are subject to feedback and correction, delusions are not. Technically, a delusion is a persistent false belief held against contradictory evidence – a symptom of psychiatric disorder. The patient who believes he is Napoleon is delusional.

I want to use the word in a non-technical sense. Understanding a delusion as a false belief fervently held against all odds.

Ideologies, typically, are delusions. The Afrikaner nationalists' belief that it was possible to create a geo-political separation of whites from blacks in South Africa was delusionary. And it led to cruel legislation preventing marriage across the colour line and the creation of separate but unequal Bantustans where blacks would, so the delusion went, have full 'citizenship' rights. Delusions are dangerous and hurtful things. But we shouldn't be misled into thinking only of political delusions.

Nor should we accept the somewhat trite use of the word 'delusion' in connection with belief in God. I'm thinking here of Richard Dawkins bestseller, *The God Delusion*. Dawkins defends his use of 'delusion' by quoting approvingly Robert M. Persig's bestselling book, *Zen and the Art of Motorcycle Maintenance* (1974): 'When one person suffers from a delusion, it is called insanity. When many people suffer from a delusion it is called religion.'

I want to talk about delusions in a more mundane way; when we look at life through distortions. And the distortion I've learnt most about on my journey concerns my 'self' – my sense of myself, or what in Western intellectual tradition is called The Self.

'Why are you unhappy?' asks the sage Wei Wu Wei (1895 - 1986). The answer, he says, is because '99.9 per cent of everything you think and everything you do, is for yourself – and there isn't one'. And it's true. There isn't one. Not in the sense that most of us take for granted, anyway. As Oliver Burkeman writes:

> Few things seem so obvious, fundamental and undeniable as the self. Whatever uncertainties you might harbour about how to live – how to be happy, how to live morally, what relationships to pursue, or what work to do – you probably retain the bedrock assumption that all these things are happening to an easily identifiable, single entity called you.

It's not only Buddhists who claim that your sense of a permanent 'you' is a delusion. Philosopher David Hume famously proposed a thought experiment: turn you attention inwards and try to find this thing you call your 'self'. He tried many times, but he never succeeded. All he found were specific emotions, sensations, and thoughts. But where was the self that was feeling, sensing, thinking? Try it yourself.

Modern neuroscience concurs: the self is not the thing that we might imagine it to be. In the words of neuropsychologist Paul Broks, there is 'no centre in the brain where things do all come together'. It's a delusion to think otherwise.

Well, then, how should we think of ourselves? On the evidence from philosophy, the humanities and neuroscience, the best way to think of the self – of what constitutes me – is to think of the self as a fiction, a construction, a story we tell ourselves. To 'empty' ourselves, as the sage said, of our self-important 'self'. To become less fixated on our sense of ego-self. To accept the ambiguity of being contingent – a work in progress, unfinished.

You get over yourself when you are able to recognise the distortions with which you look at the world. Being an egotistical self is one such distortion. As Osler says, other distortions we need to drop include ignorance, prejudice, resistance, avoidance, resentment ...

Training the mind through meditation, developing habits of the heart, to enable us to drop our delusions is not easy. We will forget, and sometimes we don't even see the delusions, we've grown so accustomed to. That's why we need the daily vigilance of vowing to drop them. This is what I think the ancients had in mind when they talked about philosophy as a way of life.

DHARMA PATHS ARE EVERYWHERE, I VOW TO WALK THEM ALL
The third Bodhisattva vow is about how fully and attentively
we live in each situation, in each relationship. Will we be clear
and compassionate or will we be sticky and distracted.
Antony Osler in Stoep Zen

Because '*dharma*' is a Sanskrit word with no good English equivalent, you have to reach for several words to capture its sense. But it's well worth the effort because it is so rich in meaning. Owen Flanagan points to its original meaning of sitting quietly and focussing on moving your life in the right direction.

In the Hindu and Buddhist traditions, '*dharma*' refers to practices that lead to enlightenment, happiness and fulfilment – The Way or *Tao* in Taoism. In essence, it means living by precepts and practices that lead to wisdom and flourishing. Owen Flanagan says: 'Dharma usefully expresses in a single word the ideas of wisdom and enlightenment.'

The Buddha tells this parable: The dharma is like a raft that you assemble from pieces of driftwood, fallen branches and other bits and pieces. Once it has taken you across the river that lies in your way, you leave it behind on the bank for others to use. In a commentary on this parable Stephen Batchelor says: The dharma 'is a temporary expedient. To treat it as an object of reverence is as absurd as carrying the raft on your back even though you no longer need it.'

Writing from within the Buddhist tradition, Batchelor goes on to say that to practice the dharma 'is like making a collage. You collect ideas, images, insights, philosophical styles, meditation methods, and ethical values that you find here and there … bind them securely together, then launch your raft into the river of your life.'

You do not have to be a Buddhist to make a collage of the guiding precepts and practices by which to live. Your *dharma* for your journey. So here's my collage, crafted over the years and open to new insights. It is my celebration of the growing sense of freedom and groundedness I have found in what I'm calling my 'secular spirituality'.

◇ I celebrate our fragile, precarious planet earth in all its secularity, its connectedness and it's evolving.

◇ I rejoice in my non-theism, recognising that there isn't a hand to hold – up there, out there. There isn't someone or something that is going to make things right for me. We are on our own and must turn the wood that arrives in our lathes.

◇ I am coming to understand my heart has reasons that only come to light when my mind is still, open, receptive.

◇ I recognise that I am responsible for the actions I take, for what I have some control or influence over. I accept that I cannot act with impunity.

◇ I know that much of my anguish and suffering comes about by wanting what I don't have, and by having what I don't want.

◇ I am committed to live compassionately, mindfully, reverently – to love justice, and to err on the side of those who are in need.

◇ I want to remain open, willing to live with doubt, paradox, uncertainty, ambiguity.

◇ I want to be part of the movement that seeks to forge a new language for the spiritual, the sublime, the joyous – for wonder. For reverence. A language that is free of theism.

◇ I am not apologetic about my secular spirituality. It's not a second cousin to the 'real thing'. The material world is not a ladder to something beyond.

◇ I cherish the love and support of my wife and family.

◇ I value the friendships I have been fortunate to enjoy.

◇ I revel in the smell of wood shavings flying off the exotic wood I'm modelling on my wood-turning lathe.

◇ I am grateful for my bookshelf teachers West, East, North and South.

◇ I celebrate lives that have touched mine and the stories that go with them.

THE WAY IS INCONCEIVABLE, I VOW TO ATTAIN IT
In the end, words and concepts fail us.
Antony Osler *in* Stoep Zen

There is no end to our speculation regarding ultimate questions about the existence of a God or gods, life after death, and the like. This vow recognises that such questions are indeed superfluous; they simply cannot be answered with any certainty. As Wittgenstein said: 'Whereof one cannot speak, thereof one must remain silent'.

Are we then condemned to silence before the Big Questions? It's an important question. And, it seems to me, you answer it differently from a Western or Eastern perspective.

Do you believe in God, Professor? Interrogated by a journalist, Einstein answered simply, 'First, tell me what you mean by God, and then I'll tell you if I believe in him.' From a Western perspective, the question of God has for millennia been defined by the monotheistic traditions. Attempting to summarise this form of theism, André Comte-Sponville puts it this way: God is 'an eternal, spiritual and transcendent being, who consciously and voluntarily created the universe. He is assumed to be perfect ... omniscient and omnipotent ... He is the Supreme Being upon whom everything depends and who himself depends on nothing.' I don't think anyone within the monotheistic traditions would dispute this nominal definition of God.

Does a God, thus defined, exist? Science cannot answer this. Nor, it seems, can any form of knowledge, if we mean by knowledge that which can be demonstrated beyond reasonable doubt. The answer, taking in the sweep of the intellectual enterprise we call Western philosophy, is that we simply don't know. We have no proof. No one does.

Belief in (such) a God is an act of faith. Pascal called it a wager – we cannot *prove* God exists, we must *bet* on his existence. Says Jules Lequier: 'People who believe they have the truth should know they believe it, rather than believe they know it. Speaking for myself, I don't *know* whether God exists or not. I *believe* he doesn't.'

All this is easier said than done, though. The roots of theism go back a long way. Theism has been dominant in Western history. What is more, theism is inextricably tied to power, and conquest – witness the Crusades of old, the expansion of 'Christianity and civilisation' during the years of colonialism and the modern day Jihadist.

Theism is so ingrained in the West that it is difficult to extricate oneself from it, let alone to imagine oneself standing outside of its reach. As Panikkar says, the 'world of theism is a universe in itself which selects its own criteria for judging what is right and wrong.' But the fact is that theisms as such do not exhaust the human ways to encounter the divine Mystery.

That's why the Buddha's unwillingness to get caught up in metaphysical questions is so refreshing. Eastern spiritualties such as Buddhism and Taoism are not premised on the existence of God. The Buddha, says Panikkar, 'does not pretend that religions give us solutions (to the Big Questions). It seeks to withdraw human beings from their wish to play the little God – to read a part not written for them. The question of the existence of God has *no* satisfactory answer.'

We're not talking here about the silence of God, it seems, but rather about a silence of the mind. It's about learning to *silence* the mind, to acknowledge contingency, mystery in the sense of inscrutability. I would far rather, along with Comte-Sponville, 'accept mystery for what it is, namely the unknown and the unknowable in which all knowledge and all existence are cloaked, the inexplicable that all explanations either presuppose or run up against.'

As I make my way in the world, I am learning to appreciate the mystery of being alive, to be grateful for the moments of awe that I experience, to develop a sense of reverence. I've taken to heart Paul Woodruff's words:

Reverence begins in a deep understanding of human limitations; from this grows the capacity to be in awe of whatever we believe lies outside our control – God, truth, justice, nature, even death ... Simply put, reverence is the virtue that keeps human beings from trying to act like gods.

I think our final vow – *The Way is inconceivable, I vow to attain it* – is an invitation to reverence.

Bibliographical notes

I want to reach the broadest possible audience, so I have dispensed with most scholarly tools, including footnotes. Instead, for readers interested in tracing sources cited or following arguments further, I have prepared these bibliographical notes. The bibliography itself contains all references with publication details.

Epigraph: The quote is often attributed to Richard Feynman, but a definite source could not be traced.

Preface: The phrase 'memories, dreams and reflections' is borrowed from the title of Carl Jung's autobiography, a book which has had a lasting impression on me.

Interlude (7-14): James Hillman's *The Soul's Code* is a lively, if maverick, take on growing up. The 'parental fallacy' is what Hillman calls the widespread belief that we are our parents' children and that their behaviour determines our fate.

It's a disenchanted world: Given my background, *Essays in Philosophical Theology*, edited by Anthony Flew and Alasdair MacIntyre, had a profound impact on me. It was my first introduction to the questions analytical philosophy asks of theological language. Questions theological discourse has great difficulty with. George Orwell's *Nineteen Eighty-Four* is a stinging critique of totalitarian regimes; one of my set books at Rhodes. Anthony Giddens's *Capitalism and Modern Social Theory* is an excellent introduction to the thought of Durkheim, Weber and Marx. Marx's incisive critique of religion can be found in his book, *Critique of Hegel's Philosophy of the Right*. On Sigmund Freud and other founders of the social sciences see the book edited by Charles Y. Glock and Phillip E. Hammond called *Beyond the Classics: Essays in the Scientific Study of Religion*. C. Wright Mill's book entitled *The Sociological Imagination* has greatly influenced me. Steve Fuller published a book on this 'struggle for the soul of science', as he called it, entitled *Kuhn vs*

Popper. Even though science is the dominating metaphor of our time, Mary Midgley's *The Myths We Live By* is a powerful reminder that we use myths and metaphors in all spheres of life, not just in religion. William Horden's *Speaking of God* was very important for me in the mid-sixties. My copy is heavily underlined. He takes on the challenge of analytical philosophy and tries to come up with a way of understanding the nature and purpose of theological language. He argues that theological language is 'convictional language' and the test of such language is whether it describes an experience that has 'convicted' you, whether it has 'gravitas', weightiness, and can be 'trusted'.

Interlude (29-40): The Red Hill community that I studied lived on what was called a glebe, a piece of land owned by the Methodist Church, and was part of my congregation. At long last there is now a good history of the Federal Theological Seminary by Philippe Denis and Graham Duncan, published in 2011. It cannot, of course, capture the human emotions and experiences we lived through in those troubled times. John Cumpsty and I published our paper in the *Journal of Theology for Southern Africa.* I suppose everyone has them, those books to which we return again and again. For me, Thomas Moore's *Care of the Soul: A Guide for Cultivating Depth and Sacredness in Everyday Life* is such a book.

Secular sources of meaning: Peter Berger's work on the sociological theory of religion, on modernization and human consciousness, and on social ethics was formative for me. And he could write in a jargon-free, flowing manner. Charles Taylor's work has also been important for me. His volume *A Secular Age* is one of the most searching studies of secularisation I know. Pippa Norris and Ronald Inglehart have written a powerful defence of the secularisation hypothesis, called *Sacred and Secular: Religion and Politics Worldwide.* They draw upon available data worldwide over the past fifty years to show that as people's sense of 'existential security' – the feeling that their survival is secure enough to be taken somewhat for granted – their religiosity begins to diminish. This secularisation process is pretty much universal. Religion persists among vulnerable populations, especially those living in poorer nations, facing personal survival-threatening risks. Owen Flanagan's *The Problem of the Soul* whetted my appetite for more. He has written on dreams, on the Buddhist idea of the Bodhisattva, on neuroscience and ethics, and more. In his book, *The Really Hard Problem*, he takes on the challenge of how to find *meaning* in a material world. Richard Holloway, former Bishop of Edinburgh, has written several popular books aimed at those who are no longer comfortably Christian. *Looking in the Distance* is for those who are searching for meaning. He has also written about a secular approach to ethics in *Godless Morality*.

Interlude (55-67): I found myself drawing on Reinhold Niebuhr's life and thought as I grappled with issues at the GSB. June Bingham's intellectual biography of Niebuhr, called *Courage to Change*, and my doctoral thesis were always at hand. Also Niebuhr's books, especially *Moral Man and Immoral Society* and his vindication of democracy called *The Children of Light and the Children of Darkness*. I am grateful to Francis Wilson, professor of economics at UCT, for drawing my attention to Charles Lindblom's wonderful book, *Politics and Markets: The World's Political-Economic Systems*. Also, Robert Heilbroner's masterly book, *The Worldly Philosophers*, was invaluable. Philosopher Susan Neiman has written extensively on the problem of evil in the modern world. Her two books, *Evil in Modern Thought* and *Moral Clarity: A Guide for Grown-Up Idealists*, are models of intelligibility. My inaugural lecture was called 'Corporate Responsibility and South Africa's Political Economy' and was published by UCT in 1984.

Toward a moral GPS: Philosopher John Gray's provocative take on modernity can be found in *Straw Dogs: Thoughts on Humans and Other Animals* and *Black Mass: Apocalyptic Religion and the Death of Utopia*. Hans Jonas has influenced my thinking a great deal, especially his *Mortality and Morality: A Search for the Good after Auschwitz* and *The Imperative of Responsibility: In Search of an Ethics for the Technological Age*. Charles Taylor wrote extensively on the making of the modern self in *Sources of the Self* and *The Ethics of Authenticity*. John Rawls is one of the most influential philosophers of my era. His landmark, *A Theory of Justice*, is still read and hotly debated. There will be other references to Stephen Batchelor; here, I'm referring to his provocative book *Living with the Devil: A Meditation on Good and Evil*. Thomas Cathcart and Daniel Klein wrote a book about understanding philosophy through jokes, called *Plato and a Platypus Walk into a Bar*. One of my favourites.

Interlude (87-107): Tony Leon, Ray Leon's son, was Leader of the Opposition in Parliament during and after Mandela's presidency. He has written of his experience in *Opposite Mandela*. Tony Leon recalls this incident in his father's life differently from the way I do. John P. Kotter's phrase 'well-placed blockers' comes from his book *Leading Change*. I wrote a case study of this venture for the Association of Commonwealth Universities, reflecting on our attempt to fit together our vision for a library without walls, with the technological possibilities at the time, plus to requisite organisation structure. I drew heavily on game theory to make the argument that competing institutions can co-operate, especially Barry Nalebuff and Adam Brandenberger's book, *Co-opetition*. Catherine Malabou is a French philosopher with an interest in the neurosciences, where plasticity is a central concept.

Looking East: Pierre Hadot's *Philosophy as a Way of Life: Spiritual Exercise from Socrates to Foucault* is a marvellous introduction to this aspect of Greek thought and practice. Martin Heidegger makes a distinction between 'calculative thinking' on which science, technology and business are based, and 'meditative thinking' – the form we use when we are thinking about thinking, about meaning, about existence. See his 'Memorial Address' in his *Discourse on Thinking*. Our own Ian McCullum has written *Ecological Intelligence*. Stephen Batchelor wrote an intriguing book early in his writing career called *The Faith to Doubt*. For a marketing approach to the fit between belief and experience see Jan Hofmeyr's 'A General Theory of Commitment' in Jan Hofmeyr and Butch Rice's *Commitment-Led Marketing*. On the incident in Gautama's life see Stephen Batchelor's *Confession of a Buddhist Atheist*. Ken Wilber's *No Boundary*, written when he was in his twenties, is a classic. Roger T. Ames and David L. Hall's translation and commentary of the *Dao De Jing* is sub-titled 'Making this Life Significant'. Stephen Batchelor's *Verses from the Centre* is helpful on emptiness and 'no-self'. For a thoroughly modern and scientifically informed discussion of the self, see Francisco Varela, Evan Thompson and Eleanor Rosch, *The Embodied Mind: Cognitive Science and Human Experience*. On the Buddhist and neuroscientific views of the 'self', I found Evan Thompson's recent book, *Why I'm Not a Buddhist*, particularly helpful. David Loy has written extensively on Buddhist social ethics in *The Great Awakening: a Buddhist Social Theory*.

Secular mindfulness practice: Jon Kabat-Zinn's book, *The Mind's Own Physician*, records his session with the Dalai Lama. On mindfulness and depression see Mark Williams, John Teasdale, Zindel Segal and Jon Kabat-Zinn's *The Mindful Way Through Depression*. On neuroscience and mindfulness see Sharon Salzberg's *The Power of Meditation*. Yongey Mingyur Rinpoche was the subject of neuroscientific research into meditation; see his *The Joy of Living*. There are some telling critiques of mindfulness meditation. Evan Thompson describes the scene in North America as 'mindfulness mania' and argues that, when mindfulness meditation is separated from the ethical base of Buddhism, it becomes a fad. Ronald Purser's bestseller, *McMindfulness: How Mindfulness Meditation Became the New Capitalist Spirituality*, provides a Marxist-like critique of the movement. Just before going to press I read Evan Cross's *Chatter: The Voice in our Head and How to Harness It*. He's an award winning psychologist working out of the University of Michigan and director of the Emotion and Self Control laboratory. He's interesting because he does not draw upon East Asian sources. A secular approach to mindfulness, you might say. I strongly recommend Lisa Feldman Barrett's book on the brain. A top neuroscientist, she summarises in an accessible way science's latest findings on the brain. It's called *Seven and a Half Lessons About the Brain*. The opening sentence of Guy Claxton's intriguing book, *The Wayward Mind*, is 'I don't know about you, but my mind has a mind of its own'. I have found Pema Chödrön's classic, *When Things Fall Apart*, really helpful on meditation practice. Martine and Stephen Batchelor have written a helpful book on the practice of asking questions called *What Is This? Ancient Questions for Modern Minds*. Sharon Salzberg is a good guide to mindfulness meditation; see her *The Power of Meditation*. On meditation and cognitive therapy, written for the general reader, see Mark Williams and Danny Penman's *Mindfulness: A Practical Guide to Finding Peace in a Frantic World*.

Living without gods: Philosopher André Comte-Sponville's *The Book of Atheist Spirituality* was very helpful to me when I was grappling with what secular spirituality might mean. Mary Warnock and Elizabeth MacDonald have written a helpful book on assisted suicide, called *Easeful Death: Is There a Case for Assisted Dying?* For those interested in pursuing the debate about God, Karen Armstrong's *The Case for God* is well worth reading. Using big data, Steven Pinker has catalogued the violence that has plagued humanity in *The Better Angels of our Nature: A History of Violence and Humanity*. Peter Berger wrote a powerfully argued book on social choice called *Pyramids of Sacrifice: Political Ethics and Social Change*. Raimundo Panikkar's *The Silence of God* made me think as few books have. In talking about the silence of God, I've drawn heavily on his book. Stephen Fry has written a lively foreword to a book which contains a discussion between the 'new atheists', Dawkins, Dennett, Harris and Hitchens. It is called *The Four Horsemen: The Discussion the Sparked an Atheist Revolution*. Tony Eagleton's refutation of the 'new atheists' can be found in his book, *Reason, Faith, and Revelation: Reflections on the God Debate*. It was Dhammamegha Annie Leatt, my daughter, sharp as ever, who pointed out that up to this point I seem to be seeing metaphysics as unhelpful, that I am dismissive of the intellectual history of metaphysics. I am not rejecting metaphysics as deconstructionists do. I draw heavily on Susan Neiman's *Moral Clarity* for my discussion of Kant and metaphysics.

Reclaiming reverence: On texture and the Dao, read Roger Ames and David Hall's *Dao De Jing: Making This Life Significant*. Francois Jullien's writings were another revelation to me, especially his *Vital Nourishment: Departing from Happiness*. Paul Woodruff's *Reverence: Renewing a Forgotten Virtue* was an important discovery for me. On morality without God, see Stephen Law's *The Philosophy Gym: 25 Short Adventures in Thinking*. Hans Jonas is really helpful on ethics in the modern world: see his *The Imperative of Responsibility: In Search of an Ethics for the Technological Age*. Karen Armstrong's charter on compassion can be found in her book, *Twelve Steps to a Compassionate Life*. The Dalai Lama's call for a 'religionless' ethics can be found in his *Beyond Religion: Ethics for the Whole World*. The Mangena's story can be found in the *Cape Times* of 24 October 2012. Niebuhr's memorable dictum can be found in *The Children of Light and the Children of Darkness*.

Interlude (185-190): For a warning about drones see Gregoire Chamayou's *Drone Theory*. My parable is based on Markus Zusak's heart-warming novel called *The Book Thief*. On negative capability see Oliver Burkeman's lively *The Antidote: Happiness for People Who Can't Stand Positive Thinking*.

Philosophy as a way of life: I've borrowed the title of this chapter from Pierre Hadot's seminal book *Philosophy as a Way of Life: Spiritual Exercises From Socrates to Foucault*. Antony Osler's *Stoep Zen* is an earthy, textured meditation, set in South Africa.

Bibliography

Armstrong, Karen, *The Case for God*, New York, Alfred A Knopf, 2009.

Armstrong, Karen, *Twelve Steps to a Compassionate Life*, New York, Alfred A Knopf, 2010.

Barnes, Julian, *Nothing to Be Frightened Of*, London, Jonathan Cape, 2008.

Barrett, Lis Feldman, *Seven and a Half Lessons About the Brain*, London, Picador, 2020.

Batchelor, Stephen, *Buddhism without Beliefs*, London, Bloomsbury, 1998.

Batchelor, Stephen, *Living with the Devil: A Meditation on Good and Evil*, New York, Riverhead Books, 2005.

Batchelor, Stephen, *Verses from the Center: A Buddhist Vision of the Sublime*, New York, Riverhead Books, 2008.

Batchelor, Stephen, *Confessions of a Buddhist Atheist*, New York, Spiegel & Grau, 2010.

Batchelor, Stephen, *The Faith to Doubt: Glimpses of Buddhist Uncertainty*, Berkeley, CA, Counterpoint Press, 2015.

Batchelor, Martine and Stephen Batchelor, *What Is This?: Ancient Questions for Modern Minds*, Wellington, Tuwhiri, 2019.

Berger, Peter L, *The Sacred Canopy: Elements of a Sociological Theory of Religion*, New York, Anchor Books, 1969.

Berger, Peter L, *The Social Reality of Religion*, New York, Penguin, 1973.

Berger, Peter L, *Pyramids of Sacrifice: Political Ethics and Social Change*, New York, Basic Books, 1974.

Berger, Peter L and Bobby Godsell, *A Future South Africa: Visions, Strategies and Realities*, Cape Town, Human & Rousseau/Tafelberg, 1988.

Berger, Peter and Anton Zijderveld, *In Praise of Doubt: How to Have Convictions Without Becoming a Fanatic*, New York, Harper One, 2009.

Bingham, June, *Courage to Change: An Introduction to the Life and Thought of Reinhold Niebuhr*, New York, Charles Scribner's Sons, 1961.

Bloom, Harold, *The Best Poems of the English Language*, New York, HarperCollins, 2004.

Bregman, Rutger, *Utopia for Realists*, London, Bloomsbury, 2017.

Burkeman, Oliver, *The Antidote: Happiness for People Who Can't Stand Positive Thinking*, Edinburgh, Canongate, 2012.

Camus, Albert, *The Rebel*, New York, Alfred A Knopf, 1957.

Camus, Albert, *The Myth of Sisyphus*, London, Penguin, 1975.

Cathcart, Thomas and Daniel Klein, *Plato and a Platypus Walk into a Bar*, New York, Abrams Image, 2007.

Chamayou, Gregoire, *Drone Theory*, London, Penguin Books, 2015.

Chödrön, Pema, *When Things Fall Apart*, London, Element, 1997.

Claxton, Guy, *The Wayward Mind: An Intimate History of the Unconscious*, London, Abacus, 2005.

Comte-Sponville, André, *The Book of Atheist Spirituality*, New York, Bantam Press, 2007.

Cross, Ethan, *Chatter: The Voice in our Head and How to Harness It.* London, Vermilion, 2021.

Cumpsty, John S, *Religion as Belonging: A General Theory of Religion*, Lanham, MD, UP of America, 1991.

Cumpsty, John S and James Leatt, 'Urban Ministry - A Programme for Our Context', *Journal of Theology for Southern Africa*, Volume 16, September 1976.

Dawkins, Richard, *The God Delusion*, London, Black Swan, 2007.

Dawkins, Richard, Daniel Dennett, Sam Harris, and Christopher Hitchens, *The Four Horsemen: The Discussion that Sparked an Atheist Revolution*, London, Bantam Press, 2019.

De Beauvoir, Simone, *The Ethics of Ambiguity*, New York, Philosophical Library, 1948.

De Beauvoir, Simone, *The Second Sex*, New York, Alfred A Knopf, 1953.

Denis, Philippe and Graham Duncan, *The Native School that Caused All the Trouble: A History of the Federal Theological Seminary of Southern Africa*, Pietermaritzburg, Cluster Publications, 2011.

Eagleton, Terry, *Reason, Faith, and Revolution: Reflections on the God Debate*, London, Yale UP, 2009.

Eliade, Mircea, *From Primitives to Zen: A Thematic Sourcebook of the History of Religions*, London, Collins, 1967.

Flanagan, Owen, *The Problem of the Soul: Two Visions of Mind and How to Reconcile Them*, New York, Basic Books, 2002.

Flanagan, Owen, *The Really Hard Problem: Meaning In the Material World*, Cambridge, MA, MIT Press, 2007.

Flew, Antony and Alisdair MacIntyre (eds), *New Essays in Philosophical Theology*, London, SCM Press, 1963.

Fuller, Steve, *Kuhn vs Popper*, London, Icon Books, 2003.

Giddens, Anthony, *Capitalism and Modern Social Theory: An Analysis of the Writings of Marx, Durkheim and Weber*, New York, Cambridge UP, 1971.

Glock, Charles Y and Phillip E Hammond, *Beyond the Classics: Essays in Scientific Study of Religion*, New York, Harper & Row, 1973.

Gray, John, *Straw Dogs: Thoughts on Humans and Other Animals*, London, Granta Books, 2002.

Gray, John, *Black Mass: Apocalyptic Religion and the Death of Utopia*, London, Allen Lane, 2007.

Hadot, Pierre, *Philosophy as a Way of Life: Spiritual Exercises from Socrates to Foucault*, Oxford, Blackwell, 1995.

Heidegger, Martin, *Discourse on Thinking*, New York, Harper & Row, 1966.

Heilbroner, Robert, *The Worldly Philosophers*, New York, Simon & Schuster, 1980.

HH The Dalai Lama, *Beyond Religion: Ethics For a Whole World*, London, Rider, 2011.

Hillman, James, *The Soul's Code: In Search of Character and Calling*, New York, Random House, 1996.

Hofmeyr, Jan, 'A General Theory of Commitment', in Jan Hofmeyr and Butch Rice (eds), *Commitment-Led Marketing: The Key to Brand Profits Is in the Customer's Mind*, New York, Wiley, 2000.

Holloway, Richard, *Godless Morality: Keeping Religion out of Ethics*, Edinburgh, Canongate Books, 2000.

Holloway, Richard, *Looking in the Distance: The Human Search for Meaning*, Edinburgh, Canongate Books, 2004.

Hordern, William, *Speaking of God: The Nature and Purpose of Theological Language*, London, Epworth Press, 1965.

Jonas, Hans, *Philosophical Essays: From Ancient Creed to Technological Man*, Englewood Cliffs, NJ, Prentice Hall, 1972.

Jonas, Hans, *The Imperative of Responsibility: In Search of an Ethics for the Technological Age*, Chicago, U of Chicago P, 1984.

Jonas, Hans, *Mortality and Morality: A Search for the Good After Auschwitz*, Evanston, Northwestern UP, 1996.

Jullien, François, *Vital Nourishment: Departing from Happiness*, New York, Zone Books, 2007.

Jung, Carl Gustav, *Memories, Dreams, Reflections*, New York, Pantheon Books, 1963.

Kabat-Zinn, Jon, and Richard J Davidson (eds), *The Mind's Own Physician: A Scientific Dialogue with the Dalai Lama on the Healing Power of Meditation*, Oakland, CA, New Harbinger Publications, 2013.

Keats, John, Letter to his brothers George and Thomas Keats, 22 December 1817, in Horace Elisha Scudder (ed), *The Complete Poetical Works of John Keats*, Boston: Riverside Press, 1899.

Kotter, John P, *Leading Change: An Action Plan from the World's Foremost Expert on Business Leadership*, Boston, MA, Harvard Business Press, 1996.

Laozi, *Dao De Jing: Making This Life Significant – A Philosophical Translation*, Roger T Ames and David L Hall (eds), New York, Random House, 2002.

Law, Stephen, *The Philosophy Gym: 25 Short Adventures in Thinking*, London, Headline Review, 2003.

Leatt, Dhammamegha Annie, *The State of Secularism: Religion, Tradition and Democracy in South Africa*, Johannesburg, Wits UP, 2001.

Leatt, James, 'Corporate Responsibility and South Africa's Political Economy: Philanthropy or the Exercise of Power?', UCT New Series No. 98, Inaugural Lecture, 17 October 1984.

Leatt, James, 'Finding a Fit Between Vision, Technology and Organisation: The CALICO Case', in Alison Rees (ed), *Collaboration in Commonwealth Universities: Three Case Studies*, London, ACU, 2001.

Leatt, James, Theo Kneifel and Klaus Nurnberger (eds), *Contending Ideologies in South Africa*, Cape Town and Grand Rapids, MI, David Philip & William B Eerdmans, 1986.

Leon, Tony, *Opposite Mandela: Encounters with South Africa's Icon*, Cape Town, Jonathan Ball Publishers, 2014.

Levine, George (ed), *The Joy of Secularism: 11 Essays for How We Live Now*, Princeton, NJ, Princeton UP, 2011.

Lindblom, Charles, *Politics and Markets: The World's Political-Economic Systems*, New York, Basic Books, 1977.

Loy, David, *Lack and Transcendence: The Problem of Death and Life in Psychotherapy, Existentialism, and Buddhism*, New York, Humanity Books, 2000.

Loy, David, *The Great Awakening: A Buddhist Social Theory*, Boston, MA, Wisdom Publications, 2003.

Malabou, Catherine, *What Should We Do with Our Brain?*, New York, Fordham UP, 2008.

Marx, Karl, *Critique of Hegel's Philosophy of Right*, Joseph O'Malley (ed), New York, Cambridge UP, 1977.

McCallum, Ian, *Ecological Intelligence: Rediscovering Ourselves in Nature*, Cape Town, Africa Geographic, 2005.

Midgley, Mary, *The Myths We Live By*, London, Routledge, 2011.

Mills, C Wright, *The Sociological Imagination*, New York, Oxford UP, 1959.

Moore, Thomas, *Care of the Soul: A Guide for Cultivating Depth and Sacredness in Everyday Life*, New York, HarperCollins, 1992.

Moore, Thomas, *Original Self*, New York, Harper Perennial, 2000.

Nalebuff, Barry J and Adam M Brandenburger, *Co-opetition*, New York, HarperCollins Business, 1997.

Neiman, Susan, *Evil in Modern Thought: An Alternative History of Philosophy*, Princeton, NJ, Princeton UP, 2002.

Neiman, Susan, *Moral Clarity: A Guide for Grown-Up Idealists*, New York, Vintage Books, 2009.

Niebuhr, Reinhold, *Moral Man and Immoral Society: A Study in Ethics and Politics*, New York, Charles Scribners Sons, 1932.

Niebuhr, Reinhold, *The Children of Light and the Children of Darkness*, London, Nisbet & Co, 1945.

Niebuhr, Reinhold, *Man's Nature and His Communities*, London, Geoffrey Bles, 1966.

Norris, Pippa and Ronald Inglehart, *Sacred and Secular: Religion and Politics Worldwide*, New York, Cambridge UP, 2004.

Ophir, Adi, *The Order of Evils: Towards an Ontology of Evil*, New York, Zone Books, 2005.

Osler, Antony, *Stoep Zen*, Johannesburg, Jacana Media, 2008.

Panikkar, Raimundo, *The Silence of God: The Answer of the Buddha*, London, Orbis Books, 1990.

Pinker, Steven, *The Better Angels of our Nature: A History of Violence and Humanity*, London, Penguin, 2011.

Pinker, Steven, *Enlightenment Now: The Case for Reason, Science, Humanism and Progress*, London, Allen Lane, 2018.

Popper, Karl R, *The Poverty of Historicism*, London, Routledge & Kegan Paul, 1957.

Purser, Ronald, *McMindfulness: How Mindfulness Meditation Became the New Capitalist Spirituality*, London, Repeater Books, 2019.

Rawls, John, *A Theory of Justice*, New York, Oxford UP, 1972.

Rinpoche, Yongey Mingyur, *The Joy of Living*, New York, Bantam Books, 2007.

Rumi, *The Essential Rumi* (translated by Coleman Barks with John Moyne), London, Penguin Books, 1993.

Salzberg, Sharon, *The Power of Meditation*, Carlsbad, CA, Hay House, 2011.

Senge, Karma Yonten, *Everyday Buddha: A Contemporary Rendering of the Buddhist Classic, The Dhammapada*, London, Mantra Books, 2005.

Taylor, Charles, *Sources of the Self: The Making of Modern Identity*, New York, Cambridge UP, 1989.

Taylor, Charles, *The Ethics of Authenticity*, Cambridge, MA, Harvard UP, 1991.

Taylor, Charles, *A Secular Age*, Cambridge, MA, The Belknap Press of Harvard UP, 2007.

Thielicke, Helmut, *How the World Began: Man in the First Chapters of the Bible*, Minneapolis, MN, Muhlenberg Press, 1961.

Thompson, Evan, *Why I'm Not a Buddhist*, London, Yale UP, 2020.

Tillich, Paul, *The Shaking of the Foundations*, New York, Charles Scribner's Sons, 1948.

Trungpa, Chogyam, *The Sanity We Are Born With: A Buddhist Approach to Psychology*, Boulder, CO, Shambhala, 2005.

Varela, Francisco J, Evan Thompson and Eleanor Rosch, *The Embodied Mind: Cognitive Science and Human Experience*, Cambridge, MA, MIT Press, 1993.

Varela, Francisco J, *Ethical Know-How: Action, Wisdom and Cognition*, Palo Alto, CA, Stanford UP, 1999.

Warner, Michael, Jonathan Vanantwerpen and Craig Calhoun (eds), *Varieties of Secularism*, Cambridge, MA, MIT Press, 2010.

Warnock, Mary and Elizabeth MacDonald, *Easeful Death: Is There a Case for Assisted Dying?*, New York, Oxford UP, 2009.

Weber, Max, 'Politics as a Vocation', in H H Gerth and C Wright Mills (eds), *Max Weber: Essays in Sociology*, New York, Oxford UP, 1946.

Wilber, Ken, *No Boundary: Eastern and Western Approaches to Personal Growth*, Boulder, CO, Shambhala, 2001.

Williams, Mark and Danny Penman, *Mindfulness: A Practical Guide to Finding Peace in a Frantic World*, London, Piatkus, 2011.

Williams, Mark, John Teasdale, Zindel Segal and Jon Kabat-Zinn, *The Mindful Way Through Depression*, New York, The Guilford Press, 2007.

Wilson, Edward O, *Consilience: The Unity of Knowledge*, Boston, Little, Brown & Co, 1998.

Woodruff, Paul, *Reverence: Renewing a Forgotten Virtue*, New York, Oxford UP, 2001.

Zusak, Markus, *The Book Thief*, New York, Alfred A Knopf, 2007.

Acknowledgements

My book has been long in the making and I've accumulated many debts writing it. It all started years ago in the study of my long-time friend, Randall Falkenberg. We talked about writing something together to explain to our children how our minds had changed as we grappled with issues of faith and politics in this troubled country. Sadly, Randall died suddenly when we had just got started.

And I would not have been able to continue without the help of storyteller par excellence, Dorian Haarhoff. He took me under his wing and tried to turn me into a creative writer. But my manuscript would never have seen the light of day without the generous help of author, Mike Nicol. He helped me to make sense of it and believed in what I was trying to do when I lost confidence.

Over a long and varied career I have benefitted immensely from two special people who took me under their wings and helped me grow. Polymath John Cumpsty, head of the newly created Religious Studies Department at the University of Cape Town (UCT), supervised my doctoral studies and encouraged me to join his staff. Stuart Saunders, legendary head of UCT during apartheid's darkest days, invited me onto his executive team and then allowed me the space to manage.

But my deepest and most abiding debt is to my wife, Jenny. When you read this book you will understand the extent to which she has stood by me throughout the nearly sixty years of courtship, marriage and deep and eternal friendship. I simply would not be who I am without her.

Our children, Chris and Annie, have been tolerant of my clumsy attempt at being a father, often an absentee one. Chris taught me never to say never and to seize the moment. I learned from Annie to push the boundaries, to embrace unknowing. They have been generous in their support of this writing project of mine.

After so many refusal letters from commercial publishers, I so appreciate Karina M. Szczurek of Karavan Press taking a chance with my book and making it a better one.

Lightning Source UK Ltd.
Milton Keynes UK
UKHW021959220123
415741UK00005B/16